Real Serious Stuff
It's What You Do

Conversations on the Dignity and Value
of Being a Small Business Owner
And the Impact of Building a Business

I0476517

Bobby Ray Burns

Published by Real Good Publishing.

Dedicated to all of the hundreds of intrepid business owners who were gracious enough to allow me to join along briefly on their journeys towards greatness.

And especially to my partner-for-life, my girlfriend, my best friend - my wife.

Table of Contents

1. Introduction

2. Part 1 – Leadership

3. Part 2 – Purpose and Vison

4. Part 3 – People and Culture

5. Part 4 – Other Stuff

6. About the Author

Introduction

Working with the men and women who start, build and run small businesses has been one of the greatest experiences of my life. My heart and my passion is with small business owners, entrepreneurs, and the entire legacy that is Small Business USA.

And, yet, the clients that I have had the privilege to coach are also based in the Canada, Brazil, Barbados, Kenya, Australia, New Zealand, Dubai, Ireland and the United Kingdom. Entrepreneurship is a worldwide endeavor. But they all share the same challenges, frustrations, and joys.

In a world enamored with corporate rock stars such as Apple, Google, and others, it is important to remember that the bulk of the world's business is made up of small-to-medium sized businesses. While the media gushes over 20-something multi-millionaire founders, most of the work being done is by nameless 40 and 50-somethings who may never become millionaires are have an IPO.

What they want, for the most part, is summed up best by the old tagline used by EMyth years ago: "More money, more time, more life."

And it has been, and still is, my great privilege and adventure to be able to help a handful of these brave entrepreneurial warriors along the journey to greatness as business leaders.

The entries complied within the four sections of this book previously lived on my business coaching blog. I have made some minor cosmetic, factual and other editorial improvements, but these are otherwise as they appeared when first published.

My hope is that this book helps you along your own journey to greatness as a leader.

June 2015
Windsor, CA

Part 1 – Leadership

So You Want To Build A Great Business

I recently read a book entitled *Now... Build a Great Business! 7 Ways to Maximize Your Profits in Any Market*. The authors, Mark Thompson and Brian Tracy, are both forces to be reckoned with in their own right and this book is a testament to their combined wisdom, experience and knowledge.

But it was the title of the book that grabbed me and the premise that won me over. In their introduction the authors state that, "This book will show you how to attract customers, keep them coming back, and have them bring their friends." Now, what's not to like about that?!

Okay, so I'm biased. I mean, part of the focus of my work is to teach other business owners how to find, make and keep great customers. And this can only be done if you are, first and foremost, a great company with a great product and a great experience. And that requires great leadership and great people.

Mark Thompson and Brian Tracy underscore and reinforce much of what I tell people. While there is much in common in this book and in my work the biggest distinction I see is that, while I focus on small to very-small businesses, Thompson and Tracy seem to be speaking to the leadership of larger companies.

What I came to appreciate was their emphasis on company culture, customer service and experience, passion, purpose, vision, mission and inspiration. For me these are the bedrock elements of a truly great business and exercising constant attention and intention to these are vital for the business owner/leader.

While there are many great business books out there, I offer this as a starting place for the conscientious business owner who seeks to create and build a truly great company, and whose purpose and mission go far beyond simply growing fast or making money.

Oh, and one other thing about this book - they contend that a lousy economy can be a great time to start (or re-start) a business! Not that's worth the price of admission right there!

Great Leaders Are Great Communicators

Every year, without fail, there will be business books vaunting the need for leadership. The qualities and traits of effective leaders are catalogued and illuminated in various degrees of detail. The methods and techniques for becoming an effective leader are hawked almost incessantly it seems. Everyone, everywhere wants to be a leader, needs to be a leader, or promises to show us how to be a leader.

However, the profound truth of the matter is that effective leadership really is vital, crucial and indispensable if a business is to grow and succeed. And that, my friend, will never wear out. But one of the key skills or qualities - I prefer "qualifications" - of a truly successful leader is the ability to communicate. Unfortunately, this seems to be the skill that is most sorely lacking in the business world and, one could argue, in many other realms in our society. But I'm not going to talk politics here!

Inspire First
Primarily, a business leader needs to communicate inspiration: while information, strategy, and ideas are always part of the message mix, inspiring a team with the essence of a vision is the predominant communicating task of the effective leader. What is also lacking aside from leaders who do this and do it well, is the teaching of this skill. And please note that it is far more than style and technique: it is spirit.

At the risk of sounding a bit impractical and romantic I have to stress that the essence of inspirational communication comes from the heart, not the head. It is comprised of vision a leader has for his business and his team and it is communicated on a level that surpasses and transcends the brain and becomes much more visceral.

One could say it is more "right brain" than "left brain", more heart than head, more inflaming than informing. Communication is key, but how do business owners who find themselves taking on the mantle of true leadership learn to be great communicators? How do they find their voice? First, they must find their purpose and passion.

Purpose and Passion

Purpose fueled by passion and lifted with a vision is a volatile mixture. What was previously corporate pep-talk or business-speak becomes a barely contained torrent of energy and incitement! When an inarticulate business owner learns to identify, channel and express their passion and their purpose, to weave the tapestry that displays their vision, the words will find their way out.

And they will find, often to their astonishment, that it is not the power of the words that accomplishes the goal, but the power in their words!

Great leaders have, almost without exception, been great communicators. Notice I did not say great speakers - but great communicators. The main address at the Gettysburg battlefield dedication ceremony was one of two hours, delivered by Edward Everett, the best-known orator of the time.

But it was the brief speech given by President Abraham Lincoln immediately afterwards that is remembered today as one of the grandest, most sublime and most moving utterances ever spoken. Everett was a great speaker. Lincoln was a great communicator.

"What We Have Here Is the Failure To Communicate."

There is never a day that goes by in any business where a failure to communicate - no matter how small - does not occur. Despite our best efforts and our best intentions it seems that not everything we say is understood - or we don't always understand what is being said. Sometimes what we meant is not what we said. Other times what we said is not what was heard. And at still other times it seems no one is really listening anyway!

The consequences of communication failure are multifold: missed deadlines, incorrect orders, wrong information, hurt feelings, bad service, a variety of inefficiencies and lowered productivity - the list is almost endless. And this is just speaking to the day-to-day functions of an average business; the ramifications of the failure for a business *leader* to communicate can range from the banal to the profound.

It has been said in many ways by many individuals that Leadership hinges on communication. It is the heart of what a leader does: communicate. It is the primary task and requirement of a good leader. And it stands to reason that effective leadership rests on effective communication. So why do many of us do it so poorly?

On a very basic level leaders must communicate on two fronts, or modes: informational communication and inspirational communication. Both are vital, both are needed, though one could easily argue that in order of precedence *inspirational communication* has primacy.

Leadership communication is less about style than substance. And it is even less about substance than it is about *spirit*. Spirit - and passion. If you, as the leader of your organization, can effectively impart the spirit and passion of your vision you will have accomplished far more than any amount of information could achieve. And this is the realm where so many leaders stall and come short.

There are many books and courses that purport to teach leaders how to "communicate effectively". They offer, many of them, valuable ideas and techniques. But the one thing no one can teach you is to have passion. And a vision. The spirit that animates you as you take on the daily challenges and struggles of being a business owner - this can't be manufactured or coached. And yet, it must be in you - real and authentic - resident in your mind, heart, and being before you can ever hope to communicate effectively on an inspirational level to your employees!

So what is a leader to do?

I suspect that the whole passion/vision/spirit thing is not a real problem for you. Otherwise you wouldn't still be doing what you're doing. The real challenge in becoming effective at inspirational communication lies in knowing *what* you want to communicate and *how* best to do that in each circumstance.

What is called for is active *attention* and *intention*: having an acute awareness of the situation and the need while possessing the conscientious intent to communicate from the heart.

"Communication is the real work of leadership." - Nitin Nohria

Write On

"Reading maketh a full man, conference a ready man, and writing an exact man." - Sir Francis Bacon

This is going to be short. I have been touching on communication and leadership for a while now and it occurred to me that written communication, while less prevalent, is still a critical skill for the effective Leader to develop.

We worry too much about using (or not using) tools such as Spell Check, or whether or not certain abbreviations or conventions are acceptable (lol!). But, as Leaders, there needs to be a primary concern that we are truly communicating and doing so effectively.

Business leaders need to make it a point to write and write often. The practice that comes from it and the discipline required to get good at it will deliver on multiple levels. And it will open new channels to do what needs to be done above all else - communicate the vision and spirit of the enterprise to the people who must embody it for you.

So... write on!

Is It Rocket Science?

Ok, so building a world-class business - a truly great business - isn't exactly rocket science. But it's no walk in the park either. Nor is it completely intuitive or obvious. If it were that simple, more business owners would have built great businesses. We would be inundated with world-class organizations and experiencing customer service that was consistently pleasing, joyful, and surprising.

But we aren't. Because it's not. That simple that is.

Yet it would appear - at least from the sheer number of business books touting the latest secret key - that building and growing a great company resides in the implementation of someone's recently developed formula. Or system. Or some "flavor of the month" approach to hyping your employees and duping yourself.

And the overarching message seems to be that this is task that has only been accomplished by a fortunate few. And some of them were just lucky. The others must have discovered the "Secret". And a few decided to write books about it so the rest of us clueless drones might get a clue.

If that sounds a bit bitter it probably is. Somewhat anyway. Because I am bothered by the fact that what has occurred in remarkable businesses throughout history, brought about by otherwise un-remarkable individuals, was neither mindlessly simple not elusively complex. It is a combination of having the right understanding of what constitutes a great company, a lot of hard work, and having a great team.

"Greatness is won, not awarded." - **Guy Kawasaki**

If I were to formulate it I could distill it down to something like this:

Great Leadership + Great Culture + Great Service = a Great Company

---

Petroglyph 2.0

Okay, so things have progressed a bit. But, really, the underlying premise is still the same: I think I got something to say that's worth sharing and I want to utilize an effective medium that transcends the transitory nature of the spoken word. So I write it. Or text it. Or blog it. Or put into 140 characters or less...

And I suppose I could carve it into the side of a rock.

My point is that the primal urge remains the same: we have something to say and we often want to share it in a more permanent fashion using a more permanent medium. And the truly ironic things is this - we often really don't care all that much if no one reads it! Case in point: as of today there are over 156 MILLION public blogs, the vast majority of which are hardly if ever read by the public. And the count continues to rise...

The single biggest problem in communication is the illusion that it has taken place. - George Bernard Shaw

So the challenge for the Leader is to find the most suitable medium or channel for effectively communicating his or her message. Additionally, the challenge is to resist the temptation to utilize the latest high-tech medium simply because "that's what everybody is doing".

There is still great (and sometimes more) effectiveness to be had using hand-written notes. Or cards. Or letters. Even whiteboards. A truly novel medium today would be a carving on the side of a rock...

Whatever your choice, be sure that it cannot be a one-off effort - repetition is the key to ensuring that the message is effectively communicated.

Beware the illusion of communication masquerading behind the latest medium du jour.

Did You Ever Stop To Think...?

I recently re-read *What Clients Love* by Harry Beckwith. It was and is a valuable and insightful book. I highly recommend it. As I do all of his books actually. I do not agree with everything he says or advocates, but probably do with about 95%. And isn't that how it often is - we find that the more we learn, the more we do, and the more we know, the less we agree on things with others.

Because we have been thinking for a while.

The problem is that the complexity of life, of business, of merely getting through the day has increased so much that it has become difficult to take time to think well. There is a bumper sticker that reads "Have you ever stopped to think... and forgot to start again?" Sometimes it seems that we have to make so many decisions on the slimmest of grounds and with questionable understanding of the consequences. We are bombarded with contradictory advice from a plethora of "gurus" who tell us how to market, how to grow, how to keep customers... so who do we believe? And why?

If everyone is thinking alike, then somebody isn't thinking. – General George S. Patton

What I think is missing for many of us are simply the time and space to simply THINK! Time to think deeply and to think well. It is a learned skill and one that far too many have abdicated to others. The problem with the "others" is that they have an agenda. And their agenda does not necessarily fit ours. The seeming irony - or disingenuousness - in me making these statements is that I think for others and I have an agenda. If it can be considered a saving grace or a mea culpa it is this: I still want you to think for yourself, for your business, for you own vision and purpose.

What I or anyone else suggests, proclaims, advocates or promotes as a truism should rightfully be subjected to thoughtful scrutiny. I don't have all the answers. No one does. Some of my answers may be way off the mark. Many people's are. So listen, thoughtfully consider, and give regular time to thought - deep thought. Hard, deliberate, and analytical thinking.

So go grab a cup of coffee...

Thinking is the hardest work there is, which is probably the reason why so few engage in it. - Henry Ford

Real Serious Stuff

I have always believed that the business of being a business owner is truly real serious stuff. The fact that small business owners make up the backbone of the American economy is staggering to consider. It is humbling to think of the millions of jobs you provide and, as a consequence, the millions of lives you support and directly impact for good - or not so good. The impact and influence of small business in this country is manifold and complex. Owning and running your business is no light thing.

And it's not all about you.

I also believe there is a difference between what I call "shopkeepers" and what I refer to as "entrepreneurial business owners". While there is absolutely nothing wrong with being a shopkeeper, the distinction lies in the vision and the intent. The shopkeeper prefers to run a business, to manage it and reap the rewards of a somewhat modest yet successful enterprise. Growth, expansion, risky innovation or diversification is not part of the plan for the shopkeeper. Stability, predictability and continued profitability are the keys.

Fair enough.

The entrepreneurial business owner, on the other hand, thrives on change, growth, assessing and assuming risk, and pushing the envelope. The vision is large and the plan is audacious. There are no guarantees, but there is great potential. These are the individuals who strive to go from start-ups to substantial concerns, from merely good businesses to great, from being a dream to a thriving reality.

This involves vision, passion, and the ability to inspire and motivate a great team for the business owner cannot do this alone. This involves leadership at its best, infused with an entrenched purpose and mission that is continually imparted and communicated. Potential profitability - perhaps even great profitability - stands as the reward. But this is only part of the equation.

A great enterprise, no matter how small, is one that provides an environment and a culture that enervates and stretches the employees, the team. A great business thrives on change, challenges assumptions and traditions, and continually seeks to better itself and its product or service. A great company knows that being big is not necessarily the goal - but that achieving and sustaining greatness is.

Leadership, great leadership, lies at the heart of the great business. It is from the influence and direction of this leadership that the culture is formed, fostered and maintained. The team that comprises a great business - for that's all a business is really: a team of people - thrives on embodying the spirit of great service. Thus we have the three building blocks of a great business: *leadership, culture* and *service.*

Everything else follows.

Your Own Journey

Success is not a place at which one arrives, but rather the spirit with which one undertakes and continues the journey." - Alex Noble

If you are an entrepreneurial business owner then you are on a journey. Yours may have just begun, or you may have started many years ago. Either way, it is a path that is unique to you and you must tread boldly, but with awareness and intent.

There are no guarantees - you know that - but there are a multitude of rewards both tangible and intangible. And in the journey you are taking many others who depend on your leadership and your vision to carry them through.

This is real serious stuff, my friend.

Thinking Hard

I often wonder what, exactly, do I want to build?

I have been thinking long and hard on that very topic. I have made some minor cosmetic changes to my website. I have refined my message.

I have done some hard thinking.

It is now and always has been my contention that a good company can become a great company - that a decent business can be transformed into a great business. And that the transformation must and always begin with the leader. For it is only through great leadership can the mundane become the sublime, can benign mediocrity be raised to the level of true greatness.

This has always been true and it has been true in every field of endeavor.

Samuel Taylor Coleridge once said that *"greatness and goodness are not means but an end."* I find it quite interesting that he couples the idea of goodness with greatness - for goodness emanates from the heart. And I believe that real greatness flows from the heart as well. Thus, it is indeed a "heart thing" that we are talking about here.

And why not? Should we not, as humans - not merely business owners - be compelled to transcend the merely functional, transaction-based nature of "doing business"? Is it so odd that we might want to create a legacy and have a lasting impact on the world we inhabit and work in? I think not.

Think hard about this. Think from the heart.

Simply Relationships

I have been on a hiatus of sorts for the last few months. I would say that it was a sabbatical, but that implies forethought and purpose. This was almost random - impulsive and unplanned. Yes, I was planning to take some time away, but I assumed it would be a few weeks at most.

Much has happened in the meantime.

I have taken this time to reconsider my focus, my purpose, my intentions and vision for my blog, my practice - this "business" that I have endeavored to build.

It is still the core and the essence of my mission, my message, to do what I can to educate, inform and inspire individuals - particularly small business owners - to strive for greatness. Not only for a great business, but for greatness within themselves. For I believe that the former must come from the latter. I further believe that a great business not only grows from great leadership (and great leaders) but must possess a dynamic and vibrant culture. And I believe that a great business exhibits a spirit of service as it's predominate hallmark.

If one believes, as I do, that all of business can be summed up as simply relationships, then it stands to reason that great businesses are run from the heart. There must be brains, to be sure. But a soul-less, profit-driven, investor-centric business is simply that and nothing more. I wouldn't want to work there and neither would you. I don't enjoy doing business with them and neither do you.

Don't be that business.

Be a leader who practices "business from the heart".

Kaizen

"What did you do today to improve your business?"

That is a question that, as the Leader of your business, you should ask yourself every night. Better yet, ask yourself every morning, "What will I do today to improve my business?"

How well the business does today – or did yesterday – has little bearing on how it will be doing a year from now, or five years from now. That is because most business owners, if they are still in business, have managed to figure out how to keep the ship going, the money flowing – but not how to keep the business *growing*!

But what you do today to build your future is what really matters at the end of each day.

Growth is not limited to revenue or physical size. Your excellence of service should grow. Your effectiveness in client fulfillment should grow. Your reputation as a thought-leader and benchmark in your industry should grow. You get the idea. But, again, this will not happen – it cannot happen – if you are not intentionally working on it.

A great business is known by its greatness. And while greatness is somewhat subjective and prone to individual interpretations, it remains a truth that a great business is recognized as such. Even if you cannot quite articulate what it is that makes it great, you know that it is. Greatness is the result of a number of factors – a clear and compelling vision, a dynamic company culture, and a passion for service that pervades every aspect of the business.

And these have to be worked on. Intentionally. All the time.

What are you doing today?

Who Are You?

It has been said that "perception is reality". I think that, in the proper context, this is quite true. It has also been said that "image is everything." That, I think, is foolish and shallow. Image without substance will soon be seen for what it is: deception.

As a business owner, however, you must come to terms with the fact that what your customer perceives about your business, your products, your service - this is reality for them. At least it is until that perception is changed either for good or for bad. Then *that* becomes their reality in regards to your business. Continually and diligently working to shape and inform that perception is your job. It's not enough for you to know that you have the best donuts in town - if a customer doesn't think so, then you don't. It doesn't really matter if you believe that your sales staff is highly trained and knowledgeable - if the prospect doesn't think so, then they aren't.

Back in 2005, Michael Levine wrote a book entitled *Broken Windows, Broken Business: How The Smallest Remedies Reap the Biggest Rewards.* The thesis of his book about business is based on a social science theory put forth in the *Atlantic Monthly* magazine in March of 1982. The article by criminologists James Q. Wilson and George L. Kelling described their theory that if something as small and innocuous as a broken window is left unrepaired, all the rest of the windows will soon be broken.

Why? Because the message conveyed by that broken window is one of perception: that no one cares and this leads to a larger sense that no one in the community cares, etc. In other words, any small indication that something is amiss and being repaired can lead to larger problems.

So what is a business Leader to do?

First, know your own business inside and out - look for and recognize the "broken windows" in your business.

Second, know your customers "inside and out"! Get to know them better than they know themselves. Learn what their real perceptions are of you, your business, and your product or service.

Third... fix the windows.

Who Really Cares?

As the leader of your business one of your primary functions is to be a nurturer. I am not attempting to be all warm and fuzzy here - nurturing, properly understood, is difficult work. It can be painful. You may get your hands dirty. And it requires patience, persistence and caring. Nurturing is not for wimps.

There are a number of things you, as the leader, must nurture: your company's culture, your employee's morale, your vision for your business, the sense of mission or purpose, the complex web of relationships between you and your employees, your customers, your vendors, your family and significant others. It would seem that nurturing, properly done, is practically a full-time job.

And it is.

While some business owners may believe they are simply maintaining the status quo of their business - keeping the ship afloat, etc. - the reality is that whether they want it to or not and whether they see it or not, their business is going somewhere and things are either growing or dying. Much like a garden, an untended business will sprout unsightly weeds of discontent, discord and dissatisfaction. Pests will begin to infest the thing causing rot and decay. That which should be thriving will begin to die away and soon the whole thing will resemble an abandoned lot instead of a garden.

Effective nurturing requires hard work, strong hands and strong medicine - and it requires a gentle touch, sensitive hands, and constant care. The good news is that the wise leader will invest in his or her staff to nurture other nurturers - managers, supervisors, team leaders - others who will take up the burden of caring for the garden of the business. Caring begets caring, and nurturing begets nurturing. The wise leader understands that he or she cannot do it all, and they cannot do it all alone. Nor should they.

Take a look at your bio. Add the word "Nurturer".

It's Time

It has been said many times in many ways, but it bears repeating: "Time is just another word for life."

All of us have been granted the same number of hours in a day. And we all have an expiration date. No extensions. No do-overs. No exceptions.

As Leaders our most valuable resource is time. As a result, it is absolutely essential that we learn to effectively and wisely manage the time we do have. As leaders in our businesses everything hinges on how well we use time. Our effectiveness rests on the effectiveness of our time use. Our productivity, our quality, our *greatness* is founded on and emanates from our ability to make the best use of our time.

"To comprehend a man's life, it is necessary to know not merely what he does but also what he purposely leaves undone. There is a limit to the work that can be got out of a human body or a human brain, and he is a wise man who wastes no energy on pursuits for which he is not fitted; and he is till wiser who, from among the things that he can do well, chooses and resolutely follows the best." - John Hall Gladstone

True mastery of life and self springs from mastering time. Once we truly and profoundly understand the priceless value of every moment of time - every moment of life - we will be on the path to making the most of the ones we have. Treasuring time for what it is - our life - will color and nuance our perspective on everything else in life.

"A man who dares waste one hour of time has not discovered the value of life." - Charles Darwin

"Dost thou love life, then do not squander time, for that's the stuff life is made of." - Benjamin Franklin

Remember that you are mortal. So seize the day.

"It's Serious, Jim."

As the owner of a small business - however you care to define that exactly - the fact is that you are engaged in some truly serious stuff!

Small businesses employ over half of all the private-sector employees in America. Businesses like yours have created over 65% of the new jobs in this country in the last 15 years. The heart of our economy and the backbone of our free enterprise system consist of millions of people *just like you!*

You may not be overly political. You may be left-leaning, right-leaning, or somewhere in the muddled middle. Nonetheless, you cannot escape the profound impact that you share when your business succeeds, grows and thrives.

Good, functioning and profitable businesses are needed to keep this country moving forward and for maintaining our standards of living. They are needed so that millions of Americans can pursue their dreams and take care of their families. They are needed in order to provide jobs for the over 10% (or more) of Americans who are unemployed or "under" employed.

I believe that when businesses owners have the desire and the vision for becoming *great* businesses, then the tenor and quality of our nation's economy, workers, and culture will become greater as a consequence.

You can be a great leader. And you can build a great business. This truly is real serious stuff.

And it's what you do!

At Your Service

The CEO should be called the Chief Exampleship Officer. What you do and how you do it will influence your employees. For good or for bad. You have probably heard of the philosophy of "Servant Leadership". As Dave Ramsey pointedly makes clear, this is not to be seen as "Servient Leadership", but "Servant".

Like Jesus was a servant. And most definitely a leader.

If I can be blunt, there is no other kind of real leadership. Your number one priority is to serve your people. Their number one priority is to serve your customers. If I can be even more blunt: if you cannot reconcile yourself with the notion of being a servant leader you are not being a leader. You're merely a boss. An owner. The dispenser of duties and paychecks.

Serving, on the other hand, releases greatness, spurs motivation and inspires, it builds loyalty and relationship.

So serve. It's what you do, boss.

Put Your Hand To The Plow

For some this may seem an odd metaphor. For others, plowing and breaking up fallow ground is a familiar task as a leader. Nurturing the growth of people, waging battle against deadly disease and weakening pests, feeding and watering - all these are the daily tasks of a great leader.

Mediocre leaders (read: ineffective leaders) do little farming. The result is little fruit. Anemic people. Sterile or diseased culture. And no other leaders.

Seasons and timing are fundamental and inescapable for the farmer. This is equally true for the leader. Farming is both back-breaking labor at times, and bouts of routine and drudgery at other times. So it is with leadership. A farmer on the weekend is a farmer still. So, too, with being a leader: leadership cannot clock out on Friday afternoon.

The joy of the farmer is an abundant crop. The miracle of planting and reaping is the exponential multiplication that results. The joy of leadership is much the same. Multiplication and abundant growth. The farmer, if he is diligent, watchful, and wise will also grow with each season of planting and harvest. So, too, will the leader - if she is diligent, watchful and wise.

Sharpen your plow. There is still ground to be broken.

Thoughts On Leadership

No general can fight his battles alone. He must depend upon his lieutenants, and his success depends upon his ability to select the right man for the right place. - *Philip Armour*

The greater a man is in power above others, the more he ought to excel them in virtue. None ought to govern who is not better than the governed. - *Publius Syrus*

Men are governed only by serving them; the rule is without exception. - *V. Cousin*

Be known for pleasing others, especially if you govern them...Ruling others has one advantage: you can do more good than anyone else. - *Baltasar Gracián*

Go to the people. Learn from them. Live with them. Start with what they know. Build with what they have. The best of leaders when the job is done, when the task is accomplished, the people will say we have done it ourselves. - *Lao Tzu*

If your actions inspire others to dream more, learn more, do more and become more, you are a leader. - *John Quincy Adams*

Where there is no vision, the people perish. - *Proverbs 29:18*

It is absurd that a man should rule others, who cannot rule himself. (Absurdum est ut alios regat, qui seipsum regere nescit.) - *Latin Proverb*

The price of greatness is responsibility. - *Winston Churchill*

Leadership and learning are indispensable to each other. - *John F. Kennedy*

The very essence of leadership is that you have to have vision. You can't blow an uncertain trumpet. - *Theodore M. Hesburgh*

Real Leaders

The question, of course, is largely rhetorical. When it comes to discussions of leaders and leadership adjectives abound: great leaders, effective leaders, servant leaders, inspiring leaders, charismatic leaders - ad nausea. And having studied the art and discipline of leadership I am often taken aback by the sheer magnitude of... well, *talk* about leaders and leadership. Yet the one core question that seems to go largely unanswered is this: What constitutes a "real" leader? Or what does "real" leadership look like?

Now don't get me wrong - I am not presuming to have the definitive answer. That is part of my own personal quest. But I do believe I have some of the pieces of the puzzle. And I believe they are embodied in a few familiar individuals that we commonly make reference to when speaking of leadership. Abraham Lincoln is one, and he happens to be one of my heroes.

A hero almost seems archaic and bit naive these days, doesn't it? Yet I cannot think of any other term to use, especially in light of Webster's definition:

1. The principal male personage, usually of noble character, in a poem, story, drama, or the like.
2. A person of distinguished valor or fortitude.
3. A central personage taking an admirable part in any remarkable action or event; hence, a person regarded as a model.

While this does not necessarily encapsulate everything that constitutes a real leader, I think that many of these traits and qualities appear in any real leader. (And the reference to a "male personage" is simply a grammatical fact: as in a hero as opposed to a heroine.) Lincoln was all of this and more. He was a man of undisputed character who found himself in a drama of historical and national magnitude. He showed distinguished valor and incredible fortitude for four, tortuous years. And he was indeed the central personage in a remarkable event. And, lastly, he was a great model.

Both his supporters and detractors admired him and mourned his passing. His life, his methodologies, his policies and tactics, have been studied and written about for over 140 years now. And he was undisputedly a great leader and the embodiment of a real leader.

So maybe the answer to my question lays not so much in an explanation or description as much as it does in a life lived.

Living Dangerously

Though not wholly original, I have always been partial to the phrase "The Year of Living Dangerously", from the 1982 film with Mel Gibson, Sigourney Weaver and Helen Hunt. While I suspect none of us will be experiencing uprisings, shootings and government reprisals, I do expect that this can be a year of opportunities and risk. But without the risk there is no value in the reward.

"Accept the challenges so that you can feel the exhilaration of victory." - General George S. Patton

This is not to imply that business is battle. It does entail a good deal of struggle, challenges and even fighting through difficulties. And the "victory" may be long in coming. But it is even more in the process itself where true victory is experienced.

Building and growing a business is, well, it's real serious stuff. Growing and developing as a leader, nurturing and fostering a caring culture, implementing and living out a spirit of service: these are the building blocks of a truly great business!

And that is what it is all about in the final analysis - having built a great business.

Being The Level Beam

Being a leader is more than simply filling a role or having a title. In business, we know this is true because of the obvious dearth of real leadership despite the plethora of C-level positions, business owners, managers and others. People who are ostensibly leaders. Because they are there and given the responsibility of overseeing others.

But are they really "Leaders"?

You Are Being Watched

In their book, *The Truth About Leadership*, authors James M. Kouzes and Barry Z. Posner discuss the reality behind the maxim, "Do what you say you will do." They point out that the truth of leading by example is a universal one and give an ancient Chinese proverb to illustrate this: *The lower beam will not be level if the upper one is not."*

It is a demonstrable fact that if you want others to act and function in a way that you desire - ways that are consistent with your shared values and vision - you must do the same. They go on to report:

"Research clearly substantiates the power of example. Cornell professor Tony Simons has investigated the "behavioral integrity" - his term for doing what you say you will do - of managers and has found that organizations "where employees strongly believe [that] their managers followed through on promise and demonstrated the values they preached were substantially more profitable that those whose managers score average or lower."

And just to further emphasize this fact, they add that UCLA Professor Donna McNeese-Smith found in her research studies that *If managers want productive employees, they must set a good example and practice what they preach."*

Sounds easy enough. But my experience with business owners - who are, in effect, managers (or The Manager!) in their own business - often fall short of this requirement for effective leadership. And they wonder why they have issues with employees. Or why their efforts to build and foster a culture of shared values and trust feel insufficient and stunted.

Often because they just ain't doing what they say.

Take Me To My Leader
Another, somewhat corollary, truth to this idea is that people WANT to be led. The resistance you may feel from employees and others is not necessarily insubordination or simply independent-mindedness, though there may be some of that lurking. But more often, it is a symptom of a larger issue - the lack of trust and belief in their leader.

Your company needs a leader, and your employees want a leader, but one that they can rely on to speak and act in integrity and transparency. One who can be 'real'. Realness in business is a virtue that is often difficult to establish and live out consistently. But it under-girds the culture and environment that fosters growth and greatness.

Are you really a leader?

Pulling The Trigger

There is a scene in the film *The Good, The Bad and The Ugly* where Tuco, the character played by Eli Wallach, is taking a bath when he is accosted by a one-armed man looking to kill him. In the now famous scene Tuco shoots his assailant with a pistol he has hidden in the suds of his bath. As his would-be killer lies dying on the floor, Tuco says, *"When you have to shoot, shoot! Don't talk."*

As business owners there comes a time in just about every facet of building our businesses where we have to stop talking and simply pull the trigger, as it were. Timing can often be critical, momentum can be at a peak, and further analysis can be counter-productive. Yet, how often do we find ourselves looking back and realizing we should have acted sooner? Or kick ourselves for not having acted at all?

We live in a time when we are admonished (and wisely so) to seek counsel, input, feedback and advice before making decisions. But this approach, while definitely good, has its own drawbacks. Namely, no reliable indicators for when enough is enough. And the fact is that, as an owner, you still have to make what are essentially unilateral decisions for your business. And you still have to be accountable for the results. Consequently, the fear many of us have of making decisions.

But, unlike the unfortunate talker in the movie, no one is going to die if our decisions are not the best. Or if we moved too quickly. And while no one will die if we do nothing, there is a good chance that your business might. Eventually…

So gather up your courage, face your fears, assess the risks – and act.

"When you have to shoot, shoot! Don't talk."

Get Real

One of the hardest lessons any great leader must learn is that no one person is good at everything. We, all of us, have strengths and qualities that, in some ways, set us apart from the mass of people. In some, these are markedly so. Great leaders recognize these in themselves and strive to improve upon them and focus them towards some greater purpose, some greater good.

But we all have blind spots. Samuel Clemens, famously known as Mark Twain, had many. He was revered as the consummate voice of mid-19th century America. His stories, tall tales, and inimitable humor propelled him to celebrity, fame, and something of a "rock star" prototype. Yet he went into his 57th year of age broke, in debt, and on the verge of bankruptcy.

According to one of his biographers, Ron Powers, he finally confessed to a business associate in a letter that year that he was not a businessman. He wrote, "I am by nature and disposition unfitted for it." Reviewing his debts, his unprofitable assets and investments, and his dismal prospects, he pleaded, "Get me out of business!"

Yet, reading through the series of decisions he made throughout his professional life, the advice he scorned or ignored, and the delusions of business acumen he fiercely held to - despite repeated evidence to the contrary - it is not hard to see in retrospect why he came to the financial brink as he did.

I want to bring out of Samuel Clemens' dilemma three key lessons that I would categorize under the rubric of "Being Real." This is a mantra of sorts that I subscribe to and is part of the Core Values of businesses like EMyth. But "being real" encompasses a wide variety of qualities and nuances.

Avoid myopic behaviors. This is not to say that a leader shouldn't be focused. But having intense focus and an unwavering commitment to a goal or a purpose is not the same as being blind to everything else.

Listen to your critics. Again, this is not to say that as a leader you should be easily swayed and dissuaded from your course or your decisions. But wisdom dictates that you must recognize your own limitations and possible misconceptions. Input, feedback, and plain ol' disagreement are very healthy.

Quantify and analyze results. This has become a tired cliché of sorts, yet it is also a fundamental and perennial truth: if you do not know what the results of your actions and decisions are and analyze them for effectiveness and impact, you cannot know if or what corrective actions to take.

Fortunately for Mark Twain, his salvation came in the form of Henry Huttleston Rogers, Vice President and Director at Standard Oil Company, then owned and run by John D. Rockefeller. Twain's introduction to Rogers was purely by chance - as these things sometimes are - but the resulting relationship, combined with Twain's new willingness to learn and accept help and advice, turned his situation around.

While most of us will never have the advantage of multi-millionaire tycoon as business adviser, we can most certainly learn to keep our eyes and ears open, and learn to recognize our limitations while putting people, tools or resources into place to compensate for them.

And have a happy ending!

Be Real

As a business owner, you may find yourself constantly being admonished to be "Authentic", to be "Transparent", or "Genuine". Another great admonition you will have thrown your way is to "Be real."

And for good reason perhaps. I mean, no one likes or trusts a patent phony. And no one - I hope - wants to be known as a fraud or insincere. Seriously, we all try to be real, to be "Authentic". But how much is too much?

Well, consider with me this: another trend that bumps up into the business newsletters, blogs and magazine articles is the need for humor in the workplace. And the onus of funny invariably falls on the leader.

Now, in the spirit of fairness, I have to disclose that I am a big fan of humor. I firmly believe that aside from working hard and making money, that if you're not having fun at what you do then you are doing something wrong. (Or maybe you're doing the wrong thing!) But being funny and being authentic can get dicey.

Bumping Into Boundaries
Take Samuel Clemens, otherwise known to the world and to history as Mark Twain. His hallmark was humor. His signature writing trait was the almost inescapable need to be funny. The preponderance of his published work is categorized as humorous - even some of his more literary and somber efforts. These were infused with comic moments and dialogue that set them apart from most other literary works.

Yet he was censored.

Literally and figuratively. His humor was his greatest marketing asset, yet he was constantly beleaguered by more pedantic and puritanical types to either tone down some of his passages or to delete them altogether. And this was not limited to his writing. Sam Clemens was a funny guy. He could almost never engage with people without saying, singing, or doing something humorous or even outrageous. Being funny - even when it offended or disturbed others - was part and parcel of his being Authentic.

When Mark Twain was "being real" he was being funny. But it wasn't always to his advantage. Nor appropriate. And that's where it gets dicey.

If you are seriously considering trying to incorporate more humor into your style, or working on being funnier as a leader - stop! A good rule of thumb is this: Be real before being funny. Because if you are not a naturally funny or humorous person then trying to be one will, by definition, negate "being real". And if your work environment does not lend itself to bouts of humor or silliness (e.g. trial attorneys or morticians, perhaps...) then it may be best to avoid that.

The bottom line is that being real trumps "being" anything that you are not. And that being your "best" self is more important.

So Just Quit

Americans hate quitting. Except for smoking, we don't typically celebrate quitters. It's ingrained in our social fabric, our mores, and our national character. The recent World's Cup race had Oracle Team USA trailing by a margin of 8-1. The New Zealand team only needed one win to clinch it. It would have been easy, almost understandable, for the Oracle team to simply give up. The odds were overwhelming.

But they didn't quit. And the rest is history.

Yet, in business, there are times when one really should quit. Because sometimes "quitting" is simply a strategic maneuver to a better position in life, a re-alignment of one's actions with one's abilities and passion.

There are three good reasons to quit if you are a business owner:

1. You're in the "wrong" business.
"Risk means everything from being honest about your faith, to moving, to quitting a job that's paying you a fortune but it's not what's in your heart. Risking things is one of the biggest fears we have." - John Tesh

Many times I have encountered well-intentioned and passionate business owners who are frustrated because they come to realize that they really don't care all that much for what they do. Their business is good and even honorable, but they wake up one day and realize that their heart is not in it - that they have no genuine passion for it. And they feel trapped.

2. You've realized that you are not an entrepreneur.
"I'm quitting the business today. I'm going to open up an appliance store; I've always really been into toasters. I'm giving it all up." - Dane Cook

Okay, so we like to think that anyone can start a business with the right product or service, a real market, and some help. But starting a business or even being a "business owner" does not an entrepreneur make! And the revelation often comes crashing in on the owner that they are not. Panic begins to set in, courses are taken, books get read, and still they find that they are not entrepreneurial –*nor do they want to be!*

3. You've achieved your vision and need to move on.
"Quitting law school was the most difficult decision of my life. But I felt this great relief that this is my life and I can do what I want with it." - Carly Fiorina

Non-profits and other organizations sometimes suffer from what is called "mission creep". They have either achieved their objectives, but can't seem to wrap it up and close it down, or they "creep" into other areas, products, services, crusades, etc. and work furiously to keep the machine running.

Business owners can do the same. But once you have "arrived", so to speak, it may be time to exercise your option to step down, move on, and do something else.

True Grit

What are the key qualities any successful business owner must possess? Vision? Passion? Ability to communicate? These are needed, but they alone do not a successful owner make.

Something more is needed. Something deep and visceral. Something gritty and not-so-high-minded.

Primal Functions

At the early stages of the American Civil War, many personages made their mark and many others were noted for their seeming rise to greatness - or descent to infamy. Among these was a relatively young general named Ulysses S. Grant.

In 1862, as a general, he fought a series of battles in the western sphere of the war and was eventually promoted to major general after the surrender of a large Confederate army and gaining Union control of Kentucky and most of Tennessee.

He then led Union forces to victory in the Battle of Shiloh. In so doing, he earned a reputation as an aggressive commander.

He was quoted at one point, when asked for his strategic secret: *"The art of war is simple. Find your enemy, hit them hard, and then move on."* Not something you may want to put on an inspirational poster with a picture of a sunrise.

Another quote attributed to Grant was this: *"If you see the President, tell him form me that whatever happens there will be no turning back."* He was admired and revered by his troops, not so much for his personality, but for his willingness to fight.

One last quote illustrates a third aspect that helped his success: *"I propose to fight it out on this line if it takes all summer."* While Grant was obviously not a quitter, he was not obstinate nor plagued with short-shortsightedness. He knew well his limitations and those of his forces. He was not careless.

The Three Traits
Although one could identify any number of desirable traits and qualities in Grant that were factors in his ongoing and eventual success, I believe there were three traits, three primal functions of his character, that both under-girded and over-arched all other qualities:

1. Commitment
2. Tenacity
3. Persistence

A truly successful business owner must possess and embody these three traits if they expect to push through the challenges and difficulties that are inherent in starting, growing and building a great business.

Commitment to the vision and mission of the business is critical. When things are at their darkest, the strength and depth of your commitment to your stated goal - your vision - may be all that is left to carry you through. And it can only come from within you. No one else can be committed for you.

Tenacity - the quality of being able to grip something firmly and hold fast. Some fitting synonyms for this trait are determination, perseverance, doggedness, strength of purpose, and resolve. It evokes the image of grabbing on to something and *not letting go.*

Persistence being "a firm continuance in a course of action in spite of difficulty or opposition." In the real world of owning and running a business, it is a given that one will encounter "difficulty or opposition." Things will happen. Competitors will always be there - and they will be active.

True Grit
The English language is a wonderful place for colorful and really tactile words. One of these is the word "grit". In psychology, grit is defined as, "perseverance and passion for long-term goals." It could be said that these traits listed could be captured and summed up in this somewhat archaic word, "Grit".

So the question to consider is this: Do you have what it takes to win?

Five Things

It doesn't matter whether you are a business owner, a manager, an employee, an athlete, an artist... a parent or a student - each of us has something before us that we are striving to succeed at.

And while these thoughts pertain primarily to the business leader, they are applicable to everyone.

1. MANAGE YOUR TIME. The Bible says that we are to "redeem the time" - make good and full use of the time we have. It also admonishes man to be able stewards of the limited time granted him. This has very real and profound importance and relevance to the leader. More than anything else, your most valuable treasure, asset and resource is your time. Use it well. Guard it jealously. Spend it wisely.

2. STAY FOCUSED. As one man put it, "Wherever you are, be there." Being present, being fully aware, having intentional focus, is the result of assiduous organization. Being organized and, therefore, able to focus allows us to experience the sense of control and undivided attention that is vital to succeeding.

3. HAVE A VISION. The human animal thrives on having purpose, goals and objectives. Whether yours is short term and immediate, or long range and grandiose, a vision is what provides the foundation for our motivation and diligence.

4. HAVE A PLAN. You will never realize your vision and objectives without one. Plans can change, but having a plan strengthens focus and guides decisions. Oftentimes, the choice between A and B is dictated by which choice aligns with your plan. In addition, there is great value that comes from the very act of *planning*. Certain areas of the brain are stimulated and strengthened when we are planning - whether the plan itself is realized or not.

5. FUEL YOUR PASSION. Superb time management, being highly organized, possessing a clear vision, and having a solid plan will only take you so far. Without a deep and heartfelt passion for the thing, you will likely never arrive there. Passion is the fuel that helps to drive us beyond the doldrums, the drudgery, the setbacks and doubts. Passion is what makes the fight feel worthwhile. Passion is the fire that keeps the vision burning bright. Stir your passion. Without it, succeeding will be simply a task accomplished.

Nothing more.

Change Or Die

It has become something of a very worn-out cliché', but the concept is still valid: a business owner must be able to innovate and think beyond their habitual ways of thinking in order to survive, to grow, to thrive. It is no surprise to anyone that the world seems to change daily. Social media, technology, cultural mores - what was accepted as true a year ago may not be true today. What worked wonders in sales when you launched your business might not be nearly as effective today.

And who knows about next year?

What does it mean, really, to "think outside the box"? For a small business owner it means, among other things, breaking out of the reactionary and myopic thought patterns that have been rehearsed and ingrained for years. It also means confronting the fear and discomfort of unfamiliar approaches and potentially risky considerations. Safe is easier. Familiar is comfortable. That's the "box".

Here are three tactics that will help you to look outside of your box:

Take Time Away. This means literally taking time - during your work day - and stop working. Go somewhere that is not your office, your shop, your store. Go outside and take a walk. Catch a bus and ride a route and back again. Go away and take some time to think outside of and away from the familiar crush of your work environment. And take a notebook...

Read Other Books. Business owners are an interesting lot when it comes to reading habits. Some consume business books and self-help books like candy. Others avoid books - all books - like dental appointments. And most make a valiant attempt to keep up on whatever business books are currently hot or have been recommended. First, if you own a business or are any other kind of leader, you have to read. Leaders are readers. Secondly, you need to learn to read *widely* and read *deeply.* Your mind, your character, and your leadership are not two-dimensional. Stretch and expand your horizons. Regularly.

Shop Your World. We've all heard the admonition to "shop your competition". You should do that, but there is far more in your world than other business owners who are probably busy thinking away inside their own boxes. Look around you at all the businesses, museums, government agencies, non-profit entities, social events, schools - your world is jam-packed with a myriad of people doing things in new and different ways, selling their products, services, causes, etc. in any number of ways, using any number of techniques, tactics, and tools. Your world is a playground of ideas, inspiration and knowledge. Go check it out, ask questions, think about it, take notes... and take it all in.

There is one other facet that needs to inform and direct these three activities. That is the approach of what I call *Attention* and *Intention*. You should purposely be acutely aware of what you are seeing, hearing and experiencing. And you should approach these with singular purpose.

In other words, pay attention not only to what you think, read, or see, but how it resonates with you, what it triggers in you, and how it connects with your world, your business, your needs. And be very intentional in your thinking time, in your reading, and in "shopping" your world. These are not simply random activities that will magically cause you to become an innovative genius.

It is work.

You Can't Fly Alone

I want to share why I am passionate about the value and necessity of coaching for business owners.

Having worked with hundreds of owners of small to medium-sized business - and interviewed many more - I can say with the utmost confidence that most owners really do not have a plan. And when they do have a plan, more often than not, it is not sufficient to carry them through to their expressed goals. Consequently, they end up frustrated, often overwhelmed, and far short of the success they have envisioned for themselves.

If you simply want to fly it doesn't take much to get off the ground and soar for a while. But if you want to accomplish a long distance flight to a predetermined destination and land safely, it will require far more than a pair of wings and cliff to leap from...

3, 2, 1... Take Off!

If we were to liken the journey of a business to a flying machine we could identify five key elements that must be in place in order for the pilot (You!) to successfully navigate the craft (Your business) to your stated destination:

1. Vision

Simply put, if you don't know where you're going then it doesn't much matter where you end up. And, if that is the case, there is little point in developing a plan. You must have a clear and compelling vision that will not only inspire you and your flight crew, but will serve as a beacon to your desired destination.

2. Purpose

This is what provides your lift - a strong and clear purpose is like the wings of your craft. Without it you may move forward, but you will not soar. You must have a deep and heart-felt reason for why you are doing what you are doing.

3. Passion

Passion is the engine that drives you forward. It is the thrust that enables your purpose to provide the lift you need to truly fly. Without a fervent passion and drive, your business will be stalled by the winds and currents of difficulty, setbacks, and drudgery

4. Money
There is nothing particularly glamorous or inspiring about gasoline or aircraft fuel, but without it you will simply be sitting on the tarmac. Cash is the fuel that makes your engine go!

5. Plan
Everything else can be in place, but without a comprehensive flight plan it is unlikely you will ever reach your intended destination. How much fuel will you need? Where and when will you need to re-fuel? Is you crew large enough? Are they the right fit for this expedition? How will you best get to where you want to be? How long will it take and what will you likely encounter along the way? What is your contingency plan and will you need reserves and emergency supplies?

You get the idea...

Help On the Ground
And this is where business coaching comes in. Any successful mission has support on the ground. A business coach can provide direction, feedback, insight, accountability and advice that all springs from years of experience supporting others and with the use of valuable tools and processes.

A **good coach** will be there as you prepare, when you take off, throughout your journey, and when you come in for your final approach. Something to consider as you contemplate where you want to go in the months to come.

You Don't Have To Be A Saint

Some people know the story of St. Patrick and most simply know he is someone we celebrate every year by wearing green and tossing off bad Irish brogues at parties. But he was a real person who lived, served, and died while still serving those he had devoted himself to.

Patrick was captured by Irish pirates, according to most sources, at the age of 16, taken from his home in ancient Britain, and sold into slavery in 6th century Ireland. After six years he believed he had a prompting from God to flee from his master and return home to Britain. This he managed to do and eventually made his way home.

What is significant about Patrick's conversion experience to the Christian faith while still a slave, and his subsequent calling as a missionary, is his decision to return to the place where he had been a slave. Despite the animosity that awaited him and the very real possibility of re-capture, enslavement, or even death, Patrick devoted himself to the care and shepherding of the Irish Christian converts he would eventually win over the course about 60 years.

3 lessons from an ancient Saint
While not everyone is certainly going to identify with Christianity or even, perhaps, a belief in God, there are still universal lessons that can be gained from this life. Here are three that I feel are applicable to every successful leader:

1. Look Outside of Yourself
You can't know everything, you can't do everything, and you shouldn't want to. We are all truly dependent on the help, wisdom, experience, insights and even frailties of our colleagues and associates. A great leader - a successful leader - knows and appreciates his or her own limitations and the need to look outside of themselves.

2. Act on Your Convictions
Successful leaders have clearly defined values and convictions. And a great leader acts on them. Consistently. And this may mean going against the majority opinion or even making decisions that place one

at risk. No matter. As a leader the need for unilateral decisions, grounded on firm convictions, is a reality.

3. Make Service Your Driving Purpose
A leader may have a multitude of reasons why they want to do what they aspire to do. But at the very heart of any stated purpose serving others must be paramount. This is not to say that a totally self-serving and ego-driven individual cannot be a leader (Charles Manson comes to mind...), but truly successful leaders, great leaders, succeed because they serve.

This is not to be confused with being 'subservient' - as a leader, you are still in charge. You are still the one who must impart a vision, set the course, and take command, as it were. But your driving purpose must be integrated with the serving of your people, your customers, and your community at large.

Happy St. Patrick's Day!
While one may ascribe any number of reasons why we still celebrate the demise of this great leader, the fact remains that his impact is felt over 1, 500 years later. There's a lesson to be learned in there.

Keep On Keeping On

"Unplanned interruptions."

That might sound a bit redundant since interruptions are, by nature, usually unplanned.

But that's how we tend to think of them: interruptions in life that are both unplanned and unanticipated. Another way to describe it might be this:

Life happens.

Keep on keeping on
Which leads me to a simple thought: "What is the real value of determination in the formula a success?"

I have come to the conclusion - one that many, many before me have also arrived at - that determination is absolutely essential. In fact, one could argue that without it, success is probably not going to be realized.

Another word for this is "grit".

A gritty view of success
Angela Lee Duckworth, associate professor of psychology at the University of Pennsylvania, has studied the implications of determined tenacity - of "grit" - in the realm of success.

She was recently interviewed in *Strategy+Business* magazine. Her conclusions apply to sports, education, and business, and her findings are both intuitive and eye-opening.

"In addition to talent," she says, "those highly successful people had a kind of staying power. They were working not only with intensity, but also with stamina over long periods of time, incrementally chipping away at some goal."

"That led me to grit."

Slow and steady really can win the race
Life - and business - can and will throw wrenches into our plans.
Passion and enthusiasm will flag. Desire and interest can wane. And,
at times, success can seem forever out of reach.

But with the right amount of grit - of stamina and a resolute
determination to push through no matter what - success is highly
likely.

Audacity And Ignorance: A Winning Combination?

Who would not agree that to endeavor to start a new business venture from scratch, from the ground up, from nothing but a vision, requires a certain amount of audacity?

Ignorance can, in fact, be a definite plus as an entrepreneur - especially the first time. What you don't know is everything that might cause you to otherwise reconsider or even decide not to do it.

And boundless confidence? Simply a "must have". This is not the self-deluding attitude that thinks being "positive" will overcome everything. Nor is it an over-inflated sense of one's knowledge and abilities. It is simply the grit and drive that says, "I can do this and it will work out. Eventually."

There's No Going Back Upstream
I recently read *Down The Great Unknown: John Wesley Powell's 1869 Journey Of Discovery And Tragedy Through The Grand Canyon* by Edward Dolnick. The story of Powell's expedition is one of mind-numbing and gripping suspense as well as a tale of one man's unlikely effort to do what should have been impossible.

He and nine others attempted what no one had ever done, with almost no knowledge of what they were getting into, and armed with absolutely none of the equipment or skills they would need to accomplish it. Pure audacity spurred the venture. Ignorance and boundless confidence kept them going when they should have by all rights given up and turned back.

And they succeeded.

Starting, building and running a business is very much like that.

So, how's your adventure going?

It's Elementary

There is always a danger of oversimplifying business success. The world of business books, blog posts and articles is full of such simplifications and simplistic formulas. Perhaps this is because of the way we are wired as humans - we tend to find great comfort in formulas, mantras, and maxims.

Three required elements for business success
I am under no delusions that simply possessing and exercising these three elements will guarantee success in a business venture. In fact, if all you have are these three things, but nothing else, you will get nowhere.

But without them nothing else will matter.

1. Vision - Okay, so this idea has been so worked over that it cannot help but to sound trite. I will grant you that. But some things are just simply true and they will never change. Gravity is always there; we will always be prone to fall. Vision must be there - without a clear picture of where you think you want to go, what it is you want to build or achieve, you will probably never succeed at building a business. I would bet you won't.

2. Purpose - Another term that has become cliché and overused. Nonetheless, if you do not possess a clear and compelling reason for what you say you want to achieve - your "Why", in the words of **Simon Sinek** - you will probably run out of determination and lose direction very quickly. I have seen this in action far too many times with coaching clients. You must have a solid purpose that you believe in. You have to know why you are doing this.

3. Plan - Well, duh! Okay, so that might not be obvious. Oh! You don't think so? Sadly, the real world says otherwise. Far too many entrepreneurs fail to plan, or - at best - they fail to plan well. Never mind all the alluring calls to spontaneity and continual innovation. These are aspects that should be integrated into a really great business culture, but it's not an operating philosophy. It is a recipe for eventual chaos and possible failure.

Isn't there more to it than that?

Yes, of course. But I will say it again: with a clear Vision, a compelling Purpose, and an effective Plan, all your entrepreneurial efforts will come to naught. And, yes, you must have a good product or service, good people, sound financial, managerial, and marketing functions, etc.

But you must always have these three.

Are You Leading Or Managing?

Okay. So that is really not a very fair question. Because the truth is, you have to do both to be an effective business owner. And let's not even get into how much of your time is spent being a Technician doing tactical work you should be paying someone else to do...

Seriously.

But the other truth here is that far too many small business owners function primarily as Managers. Not Leaders. They unknowingly build a role for themselves as the Chief Shopkeeper - keeping it going, holding it together, and putting out the fires.

But no one really knows where they're going. Or why.

Who's minding the bridge?
On a ship at sea there is always one person who is in command. Regardless of how large or small the crew is, *someone* is in charge. Someone mans the bridge.

This is not to say that the Captain (or Skipper!) doesn't get his or her hands dirty. In fact, the best ship captains pretty much know how to do everything that needs to be done on the vessel. But, much more importantly, the Captain knows where the ship is going, why it's going there, and how it's going to get there.

And the Captain knows how to delegate tasks and rely on the command structure. The Captain is a Leader. The ship's officers take care of the managing. And they all know where they're going.

Do you know where *your* ship is going?

With Great Power

There are a number of concepts and truths in business that are powerful. Actions we take, words we speak, and the strategies we employ all have power to make or break our business. But there are four aspects of leadership that matter most:

The Power of Vision

The legendary founder of IBM, Tom Watson, explained once why his company achieved the level of success that it became so well-known for:

"IBM is what it is today for three special reasons. The first reason is that, at the very beginning, I had a very clear picture of what the company would look like when it was finally done. You might say I had a model in my mind of what it would look like when the dream—my vision—was in place."

"The second reason was that once I had that picture, I asked myself how a company which looked like that would have to act. I then created a picture of how IBM would act when it was finally done."

"The third reason IBM has been so successful was that once I had a picture of how IBM would look when the dream was in place and how such a company would have to act, I realized that, unless we began to act that way from the very beginning, we would never get there."

"From the very outset, IBM was fashioned after the template of my vision. And each and every day we attempted to model the company after that template. At the end of each day, we asked ourselves how well we did, discovered the disparity between where we were and where we had committed ourselves to be, and, at the start of the following day, set out to make up for the difference."

The Power of Written Words

Tom Watson had a vision for what he wanted to create. So did Walt Disney, when he saw Disneyland in the orange groves of California, and Tony Hsieh, the CEO of Zappos.com, who saw the possibilities of delivering over-the-top customer service while selling shoes online.

And each of them wrote out their vision in some form or another. As should you.

Your written vision can become your blueprint for what you want to create. It will help you stay on track towards accomplishing whatever it is you have envisioned for your company and yourself. But without it, you are very likely to simply go along some organic and random growth path that will take you and your business some place you never imagined.

The Power of Leadership

Secondly, after envisioning a clear and compelling image of your company at, say, three years from now write down your vision. Don't worry about the quality of the writing - focus on capturing the details and the passion behind your vision. And once you have done so you can work on refining and finalizing this "vision statement" so that you have something you can then share with your entire staff.

With your vision clearly communicated to everyone in the company you can begin to consistently ask this critical question: How do we need to act every day in order to realize the vision? Asking and answering this question is one of the most important things you will do as an owner and Leader because no one else holds the vision like you do. And nobody else is charged with consistently communicating it.

The Power of Culture

The third thing Mr. Watson described was how his team acted as if they already worked at the company he wanted to create, in order to realize the vision. They fully embraced his vision and made it their own. In doing so they transformed their organization.

Your business can go from being a tiny team of disconnected employees, to banding together and acting as if you're working at the company you want to become.

Creating and building a culture that is guided by a clear and compelling vision, inspired by a Leader's passion for that vision, and supported by the structure and operational strategy to achieve that vision, is a formula for success.

So, do you know where you're going?

Failing To Succeed

Henry Petroski, in his 2006 book *Success Through Failure: The Paradox of Design,* makes the argument that true success is predicated on failure. In other words, it is essential to fail in order to succeed.

This can be troubling.

This is especially troubling to those of us who have been nurtured on success stories and the philosophy of striving for perfection. While we will pay lip service to the pat homilies about learning from failure, the truth is that for many of us failing sucks.

Success breeds failure
What really struck me in Petroski's book, however, is the phenomenon that building on success to the degree that complacency and a loss of respect for what allowed for success eventually can lead to catastrophic failure.

Building on prior successes to the exclusion of failures is dangerous. Just because it worked in the past is no guarantee that it will work on a larger scale, or in a different environment, or in conjunction with other elements. And this is just as applicable to business processes and operations as it is with bridges and skyscrapers.

What a novel idea!
Not necessarily. Many times in a business environment there is the opportunity to innovate and create systems or new initiatives that appear to be truly "new". We've never done this before and it promises to be a boon to the bottom line/profit margin/stock value/market share, etc.

But, as the authors of another great book, *BusinessThink,* point out, it pays to ask why something that sounds so good hasn't already been done?

It could be that there simply wasn't the budget, the political will, or resources to do so. But, just as likely, it was already tried and it didn't work. Unless you are willing to learn from and build upon these prior "failures" you may well be setting you and your company up for an even more spectacular failure.

Don't do it!
This is the other extreme of the pendulum: fear of failure. But, as English biologist T. H. Huxley said, "There is the greatest practical benefit in making a few failures early in life." Which, in a business life, can simply mean that failure is not always fatal (it rarely is) and that without the knowledge, experience, and analysis that can (or should) come from going through a failed effort future success is less likely.

It is ironic and sad, even, that the intrepid entrepreneur that faced the unknown, the challenges, and the failures of starting and building a viable enterprise can one day become the staid and cautious business owner. The bold innovator has now become a mere "shopkeeper".

Shopkeepers maintain the status quo and avoid doing anything that might endanger the health and profitability of the business. Shopkeepers eschew innovation for fear that something may not work. Shopkeepers resist change even at the detriment of the business.

Don't be a shopkeeper.

Failing in order to succeed
The bottom line is that in order to advance your business, improve your operations, innovate your systems, succeed with your company culture, you must make mistakes. As a coaching client said to me just this morning while describing her office manager, "She doesn't make the same mistake twice."

Mistakes, or failures, are opportunities. Make the most of them. Have a strategic approach and process for analyzing and learning from them. As Kym Illman relates in his book *The Future Is Customer Service* mistakes, problems - failures - are inevitable in a growing, moving, thriving business. And he welcomes them, especially issues with customers, because he believes that mistakes are opportunities to shine and make his customers even more loyal.

And this can apply across the board. Expect failure and then jump in to leverage and capitalize on the opportunity it offers.

Keep Your Eyes On The Road

We all tend to be myopic creatures by nature. Our minds want to focus on the immediate, the present, the apparent, and the obvious. This is the nature of the Technician in us, as we sometimes framed it at EMyth.

The problem with this approach in a business is that, if you are the owner, you can't strictly focus on the day-to-day of running the thing. You must be able to see into your future, visualize your destination, and focus on the path ahead.

Oh... and do all that while keeping a hand on the wheel and paying close attention to what is happening today, now, in the moment.

Dual vision

As the owner of your company you are, by default, the Leader. (Of course, in order to become an effective and truly great Leader you must also inhabit that role by choice and by intent!) The point is that, as the Leader, it is absolutely critical that you learn to have one eye on the present (viewed within the context of the recent past) and one eye on the future (viewed within the context of the present).

I remember taking walks with my best friend in high school and we would be talking, watching people, and so on, when suddenly one of us would ask, "Where are you going?" And, invariably, the other of us would respond, "I don't know. I was following you!"

Both of us were walking somewhere, but our attention and focus were so concentrated on what was being said in the moment that neither of us was aware of where we were headed.

Sound familiar?

Attention and Intention

These are strategic leadership qualities that are the hallmarks of truly great leaders.

Attention can be described as an awareness of not only what one is doing, hearing, seeing, or perhaps reading in the moment, but also a studied awareness of what is happening around them at that moment, the larger context of what is happening, and a consciousness of the more subtle interactions, cause and effect, and systemic consequences of what is happening in the moment.

This is not some New Age or Zen-like awareness that requires you to be attuned to the Universe. It is simply learning to be aware of and paying studied attention to what's really going on around you, because of you, and in spite of you, in your business in the moment.

Intention embodies purpose framed by a larger vision. In an ideal Leader's world, nothing he or she says or does should be random or without purpose. This does not mean that you cannot engage in casual, informal conversations, or even take some time to make paper wads and throw them at people while at work. (You should try this - it might shock the pants off of some of your staff!)

Being intentional means that the larger context of all your words, actions, and decisions are framed by and embodied within the Vision you have for your business and the heartful Purpose that fuels your Vision. A mental exercise that illustrates this would be to always ask yourself this question before you say or do anything: *Does this (action) move us closer to our vision?*

Making the boat go faster
In 1998, after another disappointing rowing regatta in Cologne, British athlete Ben Hunt-Davis and the rest of his GB Eight rowing team realized that if they continued doing things the same way, they would keep getting a lot of 7th place finishes.

So they decided to approach things differently with a new strategy - asking the same simple question with every single action they took: *'Will it make the boat go faster?* The result was that they learned sustainable, dependable techniques that helped them win the gold medal at the Sydney Olympics in 2000.

A **book** was written later on and he formed a consultancy leveraging what they learned in the process. The efforts of these men epitomize the idea behind Attention and Intention, and the value of developing a Leader's unique skill of "dual vision".

So, where are you going?

Expert Status

Two guys come staggering out of a bar late one night. They both pause to look up at the full moon hanging overhead.
One drunk says to the other, "I wonder how far that is from here?"
The other drunk responds, "I don't know. I'm not from around here."

We live in a world of specialization. It is apparent in everything from the medical profession to laundry soap. The debate among consultants, copywriters, and even marketing firms is whether it is better to be "generalists" or "specialists".

As a business owner it is deadly easy to become an expert and specialist in our own business, our own industry, and our own market. We can know pretty much everything there is to know about what we ought to know.

To a point.

Law of the instrument
Give a small boy a hammer, and he will find that everything he encounters needs pounding. - Abraham Maslow

Maslow's point was that over-familiarity and reliance on a specific tool (read: specialty) can warp one's perspective on the broader view of life and experience. This can be debilitating for a business leader. In actual practice it often shows up as a dearth of knowledge, experience and understanding about the broader world. This lack of perspective, or *context,* can literally limit one's ability to solve a problem, effectively address an issue, or overcome a challenge.

It has been shown that "non-experts" oftentimes come up with effective solutions to problems quicker and even better than "experts" in a particular field or discipline. The expert's very expertise in a relatively narrow band of knowledge and understanding limits their ability to innovate and think "outside the box", to use a cliché.

Gimme options!

Ironically, specialization also limits options. If you only see A and B, then you may not even conceive that there could also be C, D, E, and so on. This can be in the realm of systems solutions, hiring options, or even market opportunities. It's not that the options or alternatives do not exist - but that the specialized mind has difficulty perceiving them.

Even something as intrinsically creative and varied as marketing can fall victim to this. I recently got one of those value coupon packs in the mail which contained, among other things, three separate coupons for air duct cleaning and inspections. Three different companies offering essentially the same service. But here's the thing: aside from some minor variations in the font, the images, and the layout, *nothing was different in the three offers!*

Three different vendors making essentially the same offer, at the same price, in the same way, with the same tactics. "Me, too!" was written all over these coupons in invisible ink. The narrow, industry-specific mindset apparently did not allow any of these three business owners to come up with something totally different and "out of the norm" for this simple marketing effort.

Who's knocking?
It has been said that opportunity only knocks once, but that is more often a self-induced condition. Some may think in terms of the "law of attraction" while others recognize that serendipity and synergy can be initiated by our own actions, but whatever the cause, expanding one's horizons mentally and experientially will provide new opportunities in endless ways.

How many business deals have been consummated after a seemingly random meeting between two people whose subsequent conversation opened doors that neither of them would have anticipated before coming together? What new ideas or new solutions have been inspired after engaging in a new activity or visiting a new place? And how often do seemingly unrelated and disparate bits of knowledge and information come together in such a way that greatly enhances a product, a service, or an approach to a challenge or problem?

It's a big world!
The value of an expanded and deepened mental context cannot be overstated. So what to do? I suggest starting with three simple activities:

1. **Read.** Read widely and deeply, and outside of your field, your industry, your specialty. Indulge in biographies, history, and sociological themes. Push yourself to think and contemplate what you learn.
2. **Talk.** Find new people to have real conversations with. Seek out individuals who are different from you, with different backgrounds and experience. Ask questions and listen. Do more listening than talking, and when you talk, ask questions.
3. **Go.** Taking trips is great, but how about taking back-roads on the way to work, visiting shops you never frequent, joining organizations you would never normally be a part of? Go out of your way to see, hear, and feel what vast stores of experience the world has to offer you.

Expand your horizons.

Master and Commander

A common frustration among small business owners is the lack of execution or implementation of their stated goals and objectives. In fact, they may have clearly articulated their vision for their business - their Big Hairy Audacious Goal - as James Collins and Jerry Porras put it in their 1994 book *Built to Last: Successful Habits of Visionary Companies* . But too often they feel stifled when it comes to seeing this thing come to pass.

And they're not the only ones who see it; their employees do, too.

Commander's Intent
"Make it so." – Captain Jean-Luc-Picard, Commander, USS Enterprise

There is a planning concept that is used in the military commonly referred to as "Commander's Intent", or CSI or CI. It is the idea that the commander, be it a General, Admiral, or even a lower echelon officer in charge of a particular operation, will articulate a high-level summation of the intended operation. In a business context it is the equivalent of the owner's Vision Statement or strategic business statement.

Wikipedia has an entry which contains this explanation:
"Commander's intent (CSI) plays a central role in military decision making and planning. CSI acts as a basis for staffs and subordinates to develop their own plans and orders to transform thought into action, while maintaining the overall intention of their commander. The commander's intent links the mission and concept of operations. It describes the end state and key tasks that, along with the mission, are the basis for subordinates' initiative. Commanders may also use the commander's intent to explain a broader purpose beyond that of the mission statement."

So far, so good. The commander, or business owner, writes out a statement and imparts this **vision** to his leadership team, his management team, and his staff. Everyone is inspired, excited, motivated and ready for something cool to happen.

Time goes on.

A few initiatives are launched. Some processes are developed. Maybe a few new hires or capital expenditures are made. A little traction, a little activity, and then Life gets in the way. Customers need stuff. Things happen.

And time goes on.

Strategy vs. Planning
The commander's intent was based on good intentions, but something was missing between developing a strategy for business growth and the actual tools, resources and processes for making the intent a reality.

There was no plan.

The strategy was there. The vision was clear. The troops were on board. But no "battle plan" was written down and no tasks were delegated and scheduled. So nothing much got done.

And the troops got demoralized and disenchanted. The management got frustrated. And the Commander is not happy.

Plan your work. Write it down. Work your plan.
A strategy is not a plan. A plan is tangible. You can see it, touch it, read it, and pass it around. It takes your vision, your strategic intent, and makes it into a "project" and then breaks that project down into tasks. Big tasks, small tasks. And even the task of managing and overseeing the tasks.

A plan must be written down, but remain dynamic, not static. Just because you have a great battle plan doesn't mean anyone told the enemy. And just because you have a superb strategic action plan for your business doesn't mean anyone told your competitors. Or your customers. Or vendors, or suppliers, or the weather, the economy, and so on.

You must be agile and flexible while retaining your "Commander's Intent". Even your strategy may need to evolve over time, but without a plan to guide you and your staff along the way, nothing will really happen.

So, what's your plan?

"Here's Looking At You, Kid!"

We used to have a saying at EMyth that, as a business owner, you are not your business, but your business is very much a reflection of you.
I still believe this is true. And the smaller the company the more evident this dynamic is to those who engage with it.

Culture counts
As a client or a customer of a business, the perceptions we gain from our experience and interactions with that business are distinctly shaped and colored by the culture and "personality" of the business. This can be for good, for not-so-good, and even for bad.

It shows itself in the apparent mindset and attitude of the employees towards their work and towards us - their customers. It is evident in the mood, or atmosphere, of the place. It reveals itself in the quality of the service and the ease of doing business with them. It comes out in a myriad of ways, both apparent and subliminal.

And it matters.

Bad business
As a business owner it is imperative that you recognize this very real phenomenon. How people experience, feel, and think about your business is directly impacted by the culture that reigns there. And that culture - for the most part - has been dictated by you.

And you may not even know you did that!

But your attitudes, your beliefs, your values and preferences - all that makes you *you* - these are picked up and imparted to your employees, for good or bad. Your mood and your outlook on life and business set the tone for how things are done in your business. Your employees - whether they realize it or not - reflect you in what they do and how they do it.

Changing course
The good news is that with a new awareness and intentionality you can effectively change the course of your company culture. You can

alter the prevailing mindset and improve the "personality" of your business. Not because you are going to establish a "false front" on your company, but because you are going to present your best self.

We all have it and we all do it. On a first date. At a job interview. Visiting grandma. We put on our "best" self, which is nothing more than being authentic and real while intentionally keeping our less desirable traits at bay.

And there is nothing wrong with that.

So go and change the reflection in your business...

Good Times, Bad Times

It is no secret that the economy is still not doing as well as we would like. Business is hard for many. Money is tight and the future is still uncertain. Politics and party affiliations aside, it is also apparent that government alone doesn't have all the answers for turning things around.

So we wait. We worry. And we still have to run a business. Because what we do is real serious stuff.

Economic downturns are nothing new, though they are always trying times. Whether it is conditions imposed from without - recession, rising costs, lowered credit lines, reluctant buyers - or from within - major capital expenditures, costly expansions, added overhead from new hires - that challenge remains the same: How to lead the organization while keeping the vision, the purpose, and the passion alive. For it is these things that provide the fuel and the drive that is absolutely necessary during times like these.

So what is a Leader to do?

Being a role model is crucial here. While your confidence and assurance may be a bit shaken, you cannot communicate that to your employees. They will and do look to you to be a pillar of strength, a torch-bearer of the company vision, and a source of passion and purpose.

Just big words? Not really. It's nothing flamboyant; there's no hyperbole here - but there is a simple truth and recognition of human nature. The reality is that you must continue to be a role model and communicate ever more regularly, consistently and confidently while recognizing that your staff is no less attuned to what's happening "out there" than you are. They, too, have fears and uncertainties and open communication is vital to assuage those fears.

And be authentic. Be "Real".

If the news is bad and the prospects are worse, don't pretend that they're not and try to put on a front. But don't reduce yourself to hand-wringing and a "We're all going to die!" approach either. Nobody's going to die.

Some decisions may have to be made and some of them may be painful. But your employees deserve to know the truth and that you - and they - are in this together. And don't forget to balance the picture with the good news, the positive aspects, and the ever-present possibility that things will assuredly get better. They always do. And when they do your team will be that much closer, your vision, your purpose, and your passion will be that much deeper and burn that much brighter.

This truly is real serious stuff. But, then, that's what you do.

You're The Boss

It's your company, your business - you built it and sacrificed for it. It was your blood, sweat, tears and capital that made this thing possible. You did it.

Yeah, you had help. But it is your baby, and you *are* the boss.

And that's the problem...

Getting out of your own way

There are really a multitude of reasons why you should, as an owner, let go of the reins of your business and shed some of your accustomed roles. Your own personal freedom ranks high on that list. Freedom from your own self-devised "corporate bondage" of meetings, decision-making, strategizing, selling, buying, managing, firefighting... you get the idea.

Then there's your family and loved ones. Okay, so we won't even go there. (Your dinner's on the stove...)

But there are three key reasons why you should remove yourself from much of the day-to-day operations of your own business. Let's consider them briefly:

1. Money

One of the big lies that many small business owners fall for is the idea that they cannot "afford" to have other people doing the things that they, themselves, are doing. But a casual analysis will quickly show that you really can't afford *not* to hire others to do them.

Let's say for example, you as an owner were to estimate your hourly worth at, say, $250 an hour and you spend 10 hours every week doing $25 an hour work. It's costing you an extra $225 per hour - or $2,250 a week doing it yourself. Oh... and then you need to factor in the "opportunity cost" of the 10 hours of work that really only you can do, but you didn't because you were doing that other thing.

In other words, it cost you an additional $2,500 that week in lost work. So - in effect - the 10 hours you spent doing $25 an hour tasks cost you almost $5000. (You're quite generous!) And we won't even talk about the overtime you probably put in to do that high-level work anyway...

2. Time
You started your business because you wanted to be freed from, well, a boss. And from the constraints of a cubicle, or a routine, or simply the dictates of a 9-to-5 job that consumed all of your weekdays. You envisioned a life where you dictated your own schedule and had time to travel (or golf, fish, play with the kids - do stuff!)

So, where's your time? Sure, the first year or two were going to be rough. You knew that going in. Long days, long weeks, lots of overtime and sacrifice. But it was worth it to see this thing get off the ground and become a viable enterprise. It was an investment that would only be for a while.

And, yet, you're still doing it. Long days, long weeks, lots of overtime and sacrifice. But now the honeymoon is over and the glamour of the entrepreneurial start-up rush is long gone. Now it is simply work. All work. And no play.

3. Life
And it all adds up to Your Life. Ultimately, you started your own business because, in some way you may not have fully articulated back then, you wanted to have a life outside of work. Your own business was a way to enable you to be free to live a life you thought you wanted. Ownership was supposed to mean freedom, and freedom was supposed to give you the time and resources to enjoy your life.

Except that you don't. Not really.

Oh, sure, you get to take a few vacations here and there with the family. And your laptop and cellphone. You didn't have to miss *all* the games and birthday parties. But it's still not what you had hoped for or envisioned way back then.

Pink slip anyone?

Only you can fire you.

But the really cool thing about being the boss is that you can do it in phases and incrementally. You can create an action plan that provides for "coverage" - hiring new people to do some of what you currently do (that you really shouldn't be) or delegating it to others. You can implement processes to delegate, automate, or eliminate some of what is currently done in order to streamline your own work load.

Today's "To Do" list:

☐ Create a plan
☐ Write it down
☐ Begin acting on it.

You could use the money, you need the time, and your life is waiting for you.

But it won't wait forever...

Go Away! I'm Not Working.

This is a bit of musing that inspired me to ask a question that I think is both relevant and significant to effective leadership.

Okay... so the question doesn't appear to be either relevant or significant and, in fact, doesn't appear to make much sense, but I am speaking of diversions. Amusements, hobbies, activities that engage one's attention and energy, but are not work - or even have anything to do with work.

And why is that relevant? Because effective leaders need to have healthy diversions. Or, should I say, diversions are healthy and necessary for effective leaders.

I see(k) dead people.

Allow me to share one of my diversions. Although I am not a professional nor even certified in any way, I have become a pretty good genealogical researcher over the last 10 years or so. An early user of Ancestry.com and other platforms, I began digging into my family's history as a way of killing time while I went to night school. (I had lots of time to kill apparently...)

Over the course of many years of researching, digging, investigating, (and screaming and crying in frustration!) I have managed to track most of my ancestral tree back to at least the founding of this nation. Along the way I managed to uncover a number of really cool stories and intriguing characters. And the best part is that they are all related to me. They are blood kin. My family.

And, surprisingly to me anyway, was the realization that my diversion has not only broadened and deepened my knowledge of history and the world, it has taught me to be really good at research. And that's a good skill to have in my profession.

Diverting and diversions

We have all heard and read about "work-life balance" and probably have as many opinions about the idea as there are people having opinions on it. But regardless of what you may believe about "balance" for a business owner, the fact is that our brains need a break.

Taking time - intentionally and routinely - to engage in some kind of diversions is critical and essential no matter what your stage of business growth, no matter where you are in your career, no matter how indispensable you think you are.

In other words, because you are already in engaged in real serious stuff (i.e. running a business) you must be serious about taking time for things that are not serious.

So go on - divert.

Doing It For Love

People go into business for a variety of reasons. If we leave out the minority who find themselves as owners because they inherited the business, or agreed to take over for a friend or former employer (yeah. that happens...), then you have a vast majority who became business owners by choice.

And a vast majority of these business owners often wonder to themselves, "What was I thinking?"

Business Owners and The Entrepreneurial Myth
The attraction is strong and understandable. Being your own boss, making relatively unlimited amounts of money, being free to take time off whenever you want...

But the reality is often hard and sometimes brutal.

Being your own boss doesn't just mean not having to answer *to* someone else. It also means having to answer *for* everything, all the time. The unlimited amounts of money often never materialize and, if it does, the gratification falls far short of what you thought it would be. (Probably because you're too tired and work too much to enjoy it!)

This invalidates the dream of being free to do what you want, when you want.

You know it's bad when you envy your own employees and their comparative "freedom". When *they* go home at the end of the day they're really done. And there's something to be said for having your paycheck handed to you each week or two.

The myth that often pervades the entrepreneurial "seizure", as Michael Gerber called it, isn't just the idea that because someone becomes a business owner they know how to build and run a business. That's the premise of Gerber's *The E-Myth Revisited*, to be sure. But I'm speaking of the myth that becoming an entrepreneur, a business owner actually will make one happy.

Do What You Love and the Money Will Follow
Now I will contradict myself: happiness and deep gratification of life can be found in being a business owner.

The trick is to know what real happiness is, and how the business owning gig makes it happen. And while the concept of "doing what you love and the money will follow" is certainly trite and deceiving, there is also a huge element of truth to it.

I have coached owners who did not love what they did. And they had no intention of doing so. In fact, these individuals did not go into business because they loved the business, or trade, nor because they loved the process and the challenge of building a business.

No, they did it because they saw it as a way to make money. And that is one of the surest paths to frustration and unhappiness as an owner. This is not to say that otherwise well-meaning business owners are also not happy and are frustrated. But there are other reasons for this.

Making money for the sake of making money is short-sighted and mercenary. Have fun with that...

Misplaced Expectations
There are, perhaps, many reasons why business owners are not happy, but I want to point up the three main reasons that are rooted in misplaced **expectations**. And the longer one holds these expectations, the longer one will miss out on the real joy that being an owner can bring.

1. Total Ownership of Your Time
Early on in my coaching career I discovered that there are truly three consistent pain points, frustrations, and misplaced expectations that were shared by almost every client. It was so apparent in our work at EMyth that they had it in their tagline for years.

Almost every business owner knows that time is fixed, limited, and in short supply. There are only 24 hours in every day and whatever we must do must be done in the time we have available to us. And as business owners there always seems to be more stuff to be done than time to do it in.

And as business owners we get frustrated. Because we didn't really expect it. And now we resent it.

2. Potentially Limitless Money

In theory, most businesses could grow exponentially .and, if developed properly, generate ever-increasing amounts of revenue. In theory, the net profit could grow correspondingly and make the owner(s) enviably rich!

In theory.

In real life most businesses struggle to survive beyond their first few years. And, if they do, most businesses fail to make much more than the owner and a small staff can generate. Partly because they fail to grow beyond that point. Their owners cannot seem to break through that "plateau" where they are still tied to the business on a day-to-day basis.

In dentistry it's known as only being to fill so many cavities in a day. And that's where your revenue pretty much tops out.

3. Freedom to Live Your Life

This one is tied to and a direct result of the first two.

Perhaps the most commonly shared dream of first-time business owners is the vision of being able to jet off to exotic locales, or relax by their private lake whenever they feel like it. Like that's going to happen!

The most commonly shared reality of first-time business owners is the nightmare of living at work. Vacations are always something they hope to take "next year." Even relaxing by their kiddie pool on the weekends is a rare treat. And their kids have probably already grown up and left home...

This, to me, is the most heart-breaking reality of being a business owner.

It Doesn't Have To Be
But there's good news.

For most business owners, having time, money, and a life can be a reality. With properly framed expectations and the right approach to building your business, you can really find happiness and deep gratification. Your business ownership can be the source of untold emotional, mental, spiritual, and monetary blessings.

Is that over the top?

I don't think so. Because too many successful business owners can testify to the truth of it. And being a "successful" business owner is not strictly one that has made boat-loads of money. **Being rich** is more than cash and goods - it is emotional, mental, spiritual and more.

Get Help and Learn To Do It Right
Whether it is finding and working with a good mentor (or two or three!), or actually hiring a business coach, it is up to you to get the help you need so you can learn how to get free of your misplaced expectations.

If your business is drifting along a plateau with no breakthrough in sight, you can find the tools and strategies you need to make it happen. But don't give up, don't quit, and don't resign yourself to your current reality.

You can be happy!

Greatness In Leadership

There is no shortage of good books and resources on leadership. There is also no shortage of good books on how to be a great leader. But are there basic essential qualities that must be present in every leader who would aspire to be *great?*

I believe there are.

Essential Keys to Great Leadership

While there will certainly be disagreement and perhaps charges of "over-simplification" I would counter that this is not intended to be an exhaustive list of leadership qualities. But these are foundational and non-negotiable - no great leader can be great without them.

1. Vision

I know this is a term that has been overused and somewhat trivialized in the process. That doesn't alter the intrinsic value and impact of Vision. Without it, a leader is really going nowhere and is, by definition, no longer a leader - he or she just happens to be at the front of the line.

Having a clear vision of where one is going, or where one aspires to take an organization, is the probably the single most essential element of being a leader - any kind of leader really - but especially great leaders.

2. Decisiveness

This is not a call for rampant unilateralism. Great leaders elicit and give due consideration to peer and subordinate's input, thoughts, and concerns. But what great leaders ultimately must do is make decisions. People truly do want to be led, and they want their leaders to be able to make decisions - for good or bad - and stand by them. Abdication or fuzzy group politics and consensus seeking is not decisiveness.

3. Integrity

This is a powerful word with multiple meanings. And for great leaders it is used with two applications:

☐   Adherence to moral and ethical principles; soundness of moral character; honesty.

☐   The state of being whole, entire, or undiminished.

A great leader is not only one who is honest, but one who adheres to principles, one who exemplifies moral character - no matter what. A great leader is also one whose state of being is whole and undiminished. Duality of ethics or principles does not a great leader make. Someone once said that "character" is who you are when no one is looking.

A Goal to Aspire To

In the economy of business growth and the uncertainties of the free enterprise system, the creation and fostering of a truly great company originates from and is sustained by great leadership. And this means that Vision, Decisiveness, and Integrity are always at the fore within that leader.

Why Goal Setting Matters

Goal setting is certainly not a new tactic for **success**. Contrarian voices that would like to debunk the idea are also nothing new. In fact, spend a little time on Google reading up on "goal setting" (About 25,000,000 results) or setting targets (About 170,000,000 results) and you will find a plethora of opinions and approaches, both good and bad.

So I would like to contend that goal setting is a critical component of success.

"The important thing is to strive towards a goal which is not immediately visible. That goal is not the concern of the mind, but of the spirit."
– Antoine de Saint-Exupéry, Flight to Arras, 1942, (translated from French by Lewis Galantière)

Vision and Goals

When I first sit down to work with a small business client, we begin with a **Vision**. Not mine, but the client's. And it is an involved and sometimes painful exercise because most people are great with vague intentions and lofty sentiments. Not so much with detailed visions of what they want to achieve in a particular thing, at a particular time.

And that is what I require of my client's.

I ask them to describe, in writing and in detail, what their business (and their role in it) will look and be like in three years from today. The larger point of this is that the resulting Vision Statement serves as a blueprint of sorts for their "master plan" to build their current business to become what they have envisioned.

And there are three specific, tangible goals that I insist they include in their narrative:
1. A time frame
2. An annual gross revenue
3. A net profit amount

My reasoning is that, while company culture and corporate values are important, it is these three numbers that provide metrics that can be measured, tracked and documented. In addition, by their very nature these numbers will dictate, in large part, what must be built and implemented in order to make them happen.

In other words, they are Goals. They are goals that drive and direct the vision of the entrepreneur, and they are goals that will define "success" for that entrepreneur within the context of their vision.

"Goals are dreams with deadlines." – Diana Scharf Hunt

Targets are not written in Stone
One of the points of resistance that I experience from clients when engaging in the vision statement exercise is that specific targets are hard to come up with. True, but without a number you cannot really know that you achieved what you set out to achieve.

And now I will contradict myself: Moving targets are the rule, not the exception.

What I mean is that, yes, it is almost an exercise in fiction writing for a client to say, "By the end of 2017 we will be generating $5.5 million in gross revenue annually with a net profit on December 31st of $550,000." How can any reasonable entrepreneur really know what they will be earning and how much net profit they'll receive 36 months out?

They can't. But they can come up with target numbers that are both realistic and aggressive. And as they work to implement their "master plan" over the same 36 months, they can stop to review and assess their progress every quarter, every six months, and every year-end.

And they can adjust their original targets based on what they've done, what they've learned, and what has changed both internally and externally that they could not anticipate. Moving targets are simply course adjustments. They are not a repudiation of the validity of the goals that were set at the outset.

They're just simply not written in stone.

"If you would hit the mark, you must aim a little above it; every arrow that flies feels the attraction of Earth." – Henry Wadsworth Longfellow

To get to where you want to be you have to know where you're going
We are coming up on the end of the calendar year and human nature moves us to think about the future, our lives, our dreams, and... our goals.

So take the time to get away from your work, your office - everything - and make yourself dream and envision your near-term future. Seriously. Write a description of where you want your business to be in, say, three years. And where YOU want to be in relation to that future business.

Set some goals. Aim for the targets.

And in the words of Captain Jean-Luc Picard, *"Make it so."*

Part 2 - Purpose and Vision

The Pursuit Of Happiness

The word "happy" has a somewhat superficial and fleeting meaning for most people. Happiness tends to be seen as a state that is dependent upon circumstances or activities. When we have certain things (like money to spend) or are doing certain things (like watching a pretty sunset) we tend to be happy. Again, somewhat superficial and fleeting for most people. Not so surprising then that, at its root, most people's lives consists of trying to be "happy". Whether we see it as working for the weekend, looking for something fun to do or simply engaging in some pleasurable task, the goal is to achieve some degree of "happiness".

Not that there's anything wrong with this, in and of itself. But to come to the end of one's days only to find that you have spent your entire life doing nothing more than chasing momentary snatches of something we call "being happy" is somewhat of a letdown! And when we really look at the famous phrase "...the pursuit of happiness" we soon understand that the framers of the Declaration of Independence had something much more significant, substantial and profound in mind.

Thomas Jefferson, unfortunately, never offered up an explanation for his choice of words in this memorable sentence. He has been, furthermore, accused of plagiarism or, at the very least, being a bit disingenuous with this turn of phrase. Nonetheless, he and many of his contemporaries regarded happiness as a state of being that involved more than an agreeable sensation.

Happiness is bound up with the civic virtues of courage, moderation, and justice.
The 17th century philosopher, Richard Cumberland, noted that promoting the well-being of our fellow humans was essential to the "pursuit of our own happiness." And George Mason wrote in his draft of the Virginia Declaration of Rights adopted on June 12, 1776 that "all men ... have certain inherent rights... namely, the enjoyment of life and liberty, with the means of acquiring and possessing property, and pursuing and obtaining happiness and safety."

This is not to simply say that Jefferson may have borrowed his prose, but to say that he, like others, understood that happiness is the aim of life. He stated in a letter to William Short that he was "an Epicurean" - a disciple, if you will, of the Roman philosopher Epicurus. He summarized the key points of Epicurean teaching as: "Moral-Happiness the aim of life. Virtue the foundation of happiness. Utility the test of virtue."

According to Dr. Carol V. Hamilton, "When John Locke, Samuel Johnson, and Thomas Jefferson wrote of 'the pursuit of happiness,' they were invoking the Greek and Roman philosophical tradition in which happiness is bound up with the civic virtues of courage, moderation, and justice. Because they are civic virtues, not just personal attributes, they implicate the social aspect of *eudemonia* (Greek for 'happiness')."

So, how does this relate to running your business? I would ask you this in response: Does being a business owner make you happy? Are you finding happiness in what you do and what you are building? And are you exhibiting courage, moderation, justice - civic virtues - as you carry out your role as business owner? This will be seen in how you treat your customers, your employees, your vendors and suppliers, and even your community in which you do business.

In other words, is your pursuit of a great business also a pursuit of happiness?

What Price For Happiness?

So it appears that economists are interested in happiness, too. A recent report determined that after an annual income of roughly $75,000 per year, having more money makes little difference in one's sense of happiness. I can't help but to think of Maslow's Pyramid of Hierarchy and the idea that once we get beyond survival and meeting our basic physiological needs that life becomes a struggle to attain actualization.

Ok. So maybe that's a bit simplistic, but I trust you get the idea. My point is that it is here that we often become misdirected into believing that more stuff, more money, more experiences - that the best of everything or more of everything - will bring happiness.

And, that, my friend is our collective dysfunction as a society. American society anyway. I can't claim to know if this is a universal truth (though I suspect it is to some degree) but it is certainly true in the "Who Wants to Be a Millionaire" America of the 21st century. And happy we are not. Just listen to talk radio if you don't believe me.

What kind of society produces citizens who will call 911 on McDonald's because their Happy Meal was made wrong? Not a happy one. Reminds me of that song, "Looking for Love in All the Wrong Places" - we are busy looking for happiness in all the wrong things and all the while we are misled as to what truly constitutes true happiness.

If we stop and think long and quietly about those fleeting moments when we have experienced sublime and deep happiness - what were we doing at those moments? Who were we with? What was happening around us? The reality is that there was probably little going on that most of us would usually associate with happiness.

Yet we were happy. Profoundly and movingly so.

Think about those moments and begin to make THAT your life's objective.

The Intent Of Happiness

My wife and I had a discussion this morning about my current "obsession", you might say, with happiness – or, more accurately, the pursuit of happiness. In between bites of breakfast at one of our favorite restaurants (and enjoying an extended time of happiness!) she made the passing comment that if people want to have happiness in this life while working, paying bills, dealing with stuff, etc. then they need to be intentional about it.

I was struck by the sublimity and power of that thought and that word: intentional. It reminded me of a theme I have promoted for many years now that the key to much of what we want to do, achieve, have, or build in our lives and our businesses has to be the product of INTENTION and ATTENTION.

I just stared at her for a moment and then said, a bit too loudly, "Bingo! That's it! Being intentional – making the conscious and conscientious decisions to do certain things or fore-go other things in order to create and experience those moments of happiness." (This is not a normal breakfast conversation for us, by the way!)

But often times it really is a trade-off: I must give up an hour doing something that could be done in my office or in the yard in order to spend an hour playing a game with my 10-year old daughter. She's happy and I am making space for a memory and experience that will not be available for much longer. So I traded a task or a chore – which I can probably do later – to enjoy a priceless moment of simple happiness for two of us.

Short, but oh so sweet.

Purpose And Vision – Thrust And Lift

The power of purpose and the power of a vision - these are so often missing in businesses, large and small.

I was speaking with a small business owner and his wife and business partner once. She had noted that morale was slipping downward among their staff and she wasn't sure exactly what was or wasn't happening to cause this. Without really getting into specifics with them I mentioned somewhat off-handedly that having a unifying vision is often useful in this regard.

The wife jumped onto this statement with obvious intensity: "That's it, you know! That's what's missing. We really need to find a vision, a real purpose for our business."

I didn't disagree and we went on to talk about other things, but that minor epiphany that she had just experienced really moved me. How many other companies out there limp along without a compelling and inspiring vision and spirit of purpose?

What's yours?

On A Mission

I have been reading *Purpose: The Starting Point of Great Companies* by Nikos Mourkogiannis, senior partner at the consulting firm Panthea.

I have to admit that I was not familiar with Mourkogiannis until I came across this book, but the title had me on two counts - Purpose and Great Companies!

As I finished this volume I realized how much of what he says resonates with what I have long come to believe and understand: that corporate values come from a strong sense of Purpose, and that IDEAS are what allow companies to become great - not organization, systems, or structure.

Michael Gerber, the author of *The E-Myth Revisited,* refers to this idea as the Strategic Purpose of a business. I have also come to the realization that in order for an organization, a business, to have a clearly conceived and articulated Purpose, the business owner and leader must have one as well.

Purpose for the business must stem from, and be informed by, the driving and animating Purpose of the owner. At least at the start. As Mourkogiannis illustrates so well in his book, when this Purpose is lost or allowed to diminish, the company will stall and falter, as happened to IBM in the 1980's.

Purpose and Vision
Purpose is not the same as Vision either. Vision implies the future - the "What" that a company or enterprise is pursuing. Purpose speaks to the now - the "Why" for what a company does and how it does it. One can easily argue that Purpose inspires Vision which gives substance to Passion.

In a truly great company all three of these elements are actively and intentionally in play. A great company is one that is going somewhere down the road (Vision), has meaning in its activities today (Purpose), and is fueled by the belief in and appeal of both (Passion).

What's your Purpose?
Have you conceived and articulated a Purpose for your business? Is there a reason for its existence larger than simply making a profit? Is there something that your employees can give themselves to that is larger than them? A Purpose and a Vision that inspires a Passion for greatness? If not, perhaps it is time to pause and reflect deeply on just why you are in business in the first place and what you hope to achieve with your company.

Perhaps it is time to discover that starting point for becoming not just a good, but a great company!

Mission Statement On The Wall

I watched a video once of Guy Kawasaki speaking about mission statements and his preference for what he refers to as a "mantra", especially for start-ups. This got me to thinking... I wholly agree with his contention that most corporate mission statements are anything but!

He points out that for start-ups it is time-consuming and potentially costly to cobble together some buzz word-laden statement, or pay some consultant to do it for you. And the end result will not only be certain to disappoint, it will probably not be really motivating to your employees - nor will they ever memorize it, let alone internalize it! And isn't what a mission is all about?

My disagreement with Guy on this topic is his somewhat flippant statement that start-ups don't need a mission statement. While I agree that most mission statements in general are somewhat useless, the idea behind a mission statement is sound, however. A business exists for a reason - the entrepreneur or partners who started the venture had a vision and, one would hope, a mission for their baby.

The truly authentic "mission statement" then is simply a compelling expression of what that mission is. And a great mission statement doesn't have to be called a mission statement and it can be summarized in what Kawasaki calls his "mantra".

So, I wondered, what is my mantra? Educate, Entertain, Inspire? Something like that. But it could use some thought and some tweaking. In the meantime I would challenge you to come up with a mantra that embodies and succinctly expresses your true mission. And think about tossing that old one!

Business From The Heart

There is business, there is business as usual, and then there is business from the heart.

Conducting your role as a business owner from the right brain as well as the left.

Operating your client fulfillment and customer service practices through relationships with fellow human beings.

Coming from a place where your heart is engaged as often as your brain.

Seeing the people who work for you, who supply you, who invest in you, who buy from you - as people. Where adversarial is replaced with co-operative and where being a "team" really means giving, supporting, and sacrificing for others all towards a common goal, a shared vision, something larger than all of us.

What does this look like in your organization?

Does this *look* like your organization?

RISKY BUSINESS

Show me someone who doesn't dream about the future and I'll show you someone who doesn't know where they are going. " – Albert Einstein

We all want to know what the future will bring, especially in terms of our business fortunes. But we also know that the future is, for the most, unknowable. So we worry. We hesitate. We plan, scheme, plot and finagle - all the while hoping that things will work out and we will see a success with our business ventures.

The fear is that of what don't know - or can't know - about the future. The inherent risk of committing ourselves to a course of action that may not turn out well. And, yet, this is the stuff of entrepreneurship! The taking of risk. And the business of minimizing, accommodating, ameliorating and wishing hard against the risk.

So the real challenge is not so much in recognizing, accepting and embracing the risk - but in having a clear vision of just what it is you want to accomplish or achieve. It is a profound truth that if you have a vision that truly inspires you the passion that is ignited will fuel your determination to remain committed through the challenges. It is this chemistry that will embolden you take on the risk despite the possibility of failure.

No one can know if our efforts will succeed or bring financial reward. But we can know, with utmost certainty, that if we do nothing we will gain nothing. In a very real sense the future is ours to shape and mold to the extent that we can impact it. And we do this by not only our *actions* - but by our *inaction.*

It has been said that, "If you want something you've never had, you must do something you've never done."

And that is my challenge to you: Do something you've never done!

We're On A Mission

Every business exists to serve a purpose. Provide clean carpets. Deliver building materials. Serve up fresh ice cream. Any number of things. But beyond the obvious every business ought to exist to serve a *higher* purpose - to impart some intrinsic and intangible benefit or impact on the customers, the employees, the vendors... anyone who comes into contact with that business.

It can be - and often has been - argued that businesses must serve a mission, or purpose, that goes beyond mere commercial transactions. It may as simple as making people's life a bit simpler, or as profound as providing a device that makes people's life last longer. Perhaps it's little more than easing a burden, providing a solution, or enhancing an experience. Whatever your company's "higher purpose" it cannot be clearly expressed and served if it is not clearly communicated and understood.

Employees *will* give themselves to something beyond a regular paycheck and medical benefits. People do want to be a part of something bigger than themselves, and something more influential than facilitating an exchange of goods or services. Although it may a stretch to expect a small business to provide the means and opportunity for individual employees to achieve complete self-actualization, it is not at all a stretch to expect these same firms to be a place where people can find deep affirmation and fulfilling gratification. And the result of this experience, this culture, this atmosphere, is a loyalty that far exceeds that of a typical employee.

So your mission, should you decide to accept it, is to determine what the "mission", or purpose, of your business truly is. Stretch. Go beyond the apparent, the obvious. Reach into your own heart and think on what you truly enjoy most about what your business does. What is it that inspires you, motivates you, and brings you the deepest satisfaction? I suspect it isn't simply more revenue...

Coming Soon To A Theater Near You

I was thinking about the power and appeal of movie previews after coming across some of the latest on YouTube. Why is it that we seem to so enjoy watching previews? What is it about seeing glimpses of a story that captivate us so much? (And why is it that so many previews seem to have all the best scenes in an otherwise mediocre film?) Anyway, I was thinking about this in between an absurdly long stretch of watching numerous previews.

There is a similar power in a well-crafted vision statement.

Looking at your business and what you envision it to be like in, say, five years from now - what are the highlights? What are the stirring aspects and exceptionally captivating points of differentiation? How would you pitch it if it were indeed a movie-in-the-making? This is what a vision statement should provide for its audience: a powerful, heartening, inspiring thumbnail of a grand epic!

A riveting description of your future business will provide the impetus, the inspiration and the illumination your employees need to embrace and share your vision. And that is why not only drafting your vision is absolutely essential, but sharing it with your staff and integrating it into the fabric of your company culture and mindset.

A vision statement can be called any number of things. In fact, the typical "vision statement" is often nothing more than an exercise in corporate clichés, which is why calling yours something else might be a good idea.

And your "vision" should not be confused with your "mission". Your vision is your future, what you striving to build. Your mission, or purpose, is what your organization strives to accomplish each day. Both are necessary and both must emanate from the business leader.

Your business? Your vision. Your company? Your purpose.

Good business leaders create a vision, articulate the vision, passionately own the vision, and relentlessly drive it to completion. - Jack Welch

Getting There

When do you know that your business has "arrived"? In other words, aside from some compelling vision that you may have written down at some point three, four or five years ago (which, hopefully, you did!), how do you know you have built your business to the place and size it should be?

Growth often seems to be a given in our business culture. Growth-driven goals and strategies are the mainstay of the American business mindset. But is it always necessary to pursue growth for growth's sake? In fact, is it always the best strategy for every business to consistently be pursuing growth?

Is it the best strategy for *your* business?

Eight years ago Bo Burlingham, Editor at Large of Inc. magazine, wrote a wonderful book entitled *Small Giants: Companies That Choose to Be Great Instead of Big*. His premise is that growth can manifest in many other forms aside from size and gross sales. Many business owners have intentionally chosen to pursue a path of excellence and greatness in lieu of simply being bigger. Sometimes even in lieu of simply making more money.

Five years later, technology consultant Phil Simon, wrote a book called *The New Small: How a New Breed of Small Businesses is Harnessing the Power of Emerging Technologies*.

For that book, Bo Burlingham wrote a blurb in which he stated: *"We've known for a while that 'small is the new big', to quote Seth Godin, but a piece has been missing – specifically the piece that explains how technology has been accelerating the trend and how companies can harness technology to take advantage of it... Phil Simon does a masterful job of filling that void."*

So we have arrived at a point in our culture, our society and our level of accessible technology that being a small, but significantly great and profitable business is not only a preferred strategy for many owners, it is now manifestly doable.

What is your vision? To get big – or to be great?

Right Here, Right Now

I recently re-read *The Advantage: Why Organizational Health Trumps Everything Else in Business*, by Patrick Lencioni. This is a book I definitely recommend.

As I finished this book I realized that everything he says resonates with what I have long come to believe and understand about building a great business. And, in particular, I was struck by the concept that corporate values come from a strong sense of Purpose, and that ideas are what allow companies to become great – not organization, systems, or structure.

Purpose for the business must stem from and be informed by the driving and animating Purpose of the owner (or Leadership Team, in Lencioni's take on this.) And the Purpose must be continually upheld and communicated, for if the Purpose is lost or allowed to diminish, the company will stall and falter, as happened to IBM in the 1980's.

Here is Lencioni explaining the nature of an organization's purpose:

"An organization's core purpose - why it exists - has to be completely idealistic. I can't reiterate this enough. Many leadership teams struggle with this, afraid that what they come up with will seem too grand or aspirational. Of course, that's the whole point: employees in every organization, and at every level, need to know that at the heart of what they do lie something grand and aspirational. They're well aware that ultimately it will boil down to tangible, tactical activities."

Have you conceived and articulated a Purpose for your business? Is there a reason for its existence larger than simply making a profit? Is there something that your employees can give themselves to that is larger than themselves? If not, perhaps it is time to pause and reflect deeply on just why you are in business in the first place and what you hope to achieve with your company.

Perhaps it is time to discover that starting point for becoming a Great company!

Getting Clear

Everybody has a story. A purpose. A mission - a reason for doing what they do.

If you are a business owner – an *entrepreneur* - you probably have a very compelling reason for doing what you do. And it's not simply about making money. Face it: there are easier ways to make money...

No, there is something much deeper and much more compelling that comes from the heart. It is that something that stirs you to get up every morning and wade back into the fray. It is that little emotional engine that keeps you striving for that thing you have envisioned as "success". And, for some, it is the fire inside that urges you to aspire to greatness.

The problem is that too many business owners never tap into that reason. In fact, too many are not even clear as to what that reason - that purpose - really is. And they suffer as a result.

Clarity of purpose and refinement of mental focus are the keys to attaining success and greatness.

Define Your "Why"
The need is for you to literally sit down, think - for as long as it takes - and write down your story, your mission, purpose, vision. Write down your "Why", and then be ready to share it. From the heart.

This is not an exercise or a workshop activity to simply stir your juices and get you motivated. In fact, allow me to overstate the case by saying that it is a "life or death" decision. It can mean the "life" or "death" of your business enterprise, your dream.

The idea is to be able to clearly and passionately tell someone who doesn't know you or your business why you do what you do and what your mission is in doing it.

Can you do that?

Press On!

"Nothing in the world can take the place of persistence. Talent will not; nothing is more common than unsuccessful men with talent. Genius will not; unrewarded genius is almost a proverb. Education will not; the world is full of educated derelicts. Persistence and determination alone are omnipotent. The slogan Press On! has solved and always will solve the problems of the human race."
– Calvin Coolidge

There is no suitable alternative to business success for persistence. Capital, skill, market conditions, a great product, and great service - these are all necessary, yes - but if you do not keep at it, if you don't *stay in the game* - it's not going to happen.

Rule No. 1 - Being There
Much is said about having a singular focus and clarity of vision. And it is true: you gotta have that to build your business, your culture, your legacy. But it is in the grind and the periodic drudgery of a daily slog and occasional pitched battles that the tendency to drift is most apparent. We tend to lose sight of where we are going and why we are even going there.

We cease being there.

Oh, we are there in body. In fact, often far too much and for too long. 12 or 14 hour days, seven days a week might be inspiring and heroic in your start-up phase... but not after you've been at it for four or five years. So the danger is in becoming mentally and emotionally detached from your Vision, your Purpose, and your Passion.

You show up. You work. You do the things that must be done. But you aren't really "there".

So what to do?

Back to Foundations
Every business owner, every entrepreneur, CEO, etc. should, nay - *must*- be intentional about going back to his or her vision, purpose and passion. These intangible, yet foundational realities are what not

only should energize, motivate and inspire you, but serve to center and anchor you again and again.

This may mean taking a day (or three!) for a self-initiated "Executive retreat" and revisiting the reasons why you chose to do this thing, what you hoped to accomplish, and what your legacy will be when you succeed. This is not simply some "time off" to recharge your batteries. This is intentional, strategic, and focused. It's getting back to "being there".

Find some external inspiration and motivation. Biographies of great men and women have moved many to achieve great things themselves. Volunteering in some capacity to work with disadvantaged individuals can often stir us. Coaching or mentoring another fledgling entrepreneur is a great way to stoke your own fire.

Woody Allen famously and humorously said that "Eighty percent of success is showing up." Perhaps, but that being so, the critical 20% is in being there.

What Do You Do?

I am a huge believer and proponent of asking - and answering - the question of "Why?" As in, "Why do I do this?", "Why am I in this business?" and so forth. It is absolutely essential for every owner to do this.

And if you haven't yet you need to!

Asking another question
But there is another, perhaps equally important, question you should be asking yourself: *What* are you doing? And here's a bit of a spoiler alert - the answer is *not* "making widgets", or "selling a service".

That may be what you are doing on a purely functional and even transaction level, but when we transcend that and move into the meta-realm of entrepreneurial activity you have to ask yourself - really every day - what it is that you are really doing, really accomplishing, really impacting.

Making a dent
"We're here to put a dent in the universe. Otherwise why else even be here?" — Steve Jobs

While Steve didn't reference other human beings specifically, it is inherent in the statement. And it is true for you and me, as well. What we do in our daily business functions and operations involves and impacts scores of other human beings both within our organizations and without.

Nick Morgan wrote a great book, *Give Your Speech, Change The World*, the title of which serves as a great example of what I am getting at. For some it may be as simple as "Improving lives, one client at a time." or "Increasing the quality of service in my customer's business."

And yours will be specific and unique to you and your vision and mission.

What Vision?

The danger is that we lose sight of the "Why?" in the crush and rush of the business day and work. And when we function and act outside of that meta-realm of our purpose, our mission, and our values and passion, then we risk failing to "achieve what we want to" each day. We don't "do" what were meant to do. We become reactionary, pedestrian, and unremarkable.

And we run the risk of simply going through the motions and doing a job.

And that's not why you do what you do.

Is it?

Going Somewhere?

Do you even have a vision for your business?
Okay, so that may be a "Duh!" kind of question, but is it really? In other words, have you sat down and put on paper - in clear and compelling detail - what you want to have built in, say, three years from now? What is your big, meta-goal for three years from now? And can you share it clearly and succinctly?

Well, you need to.

"Would you tell me, please, which way I ought to go from here?"
"That depends a good deal on where you want to get to," said the Cat.
"I don't much care where--" said Alice.
"Then it doesn't matter which way you go," said the Cat.
"--so long as I get SOMEWHERE," Alice added as an explanation.
"Oh, you're sure to do that," said the Cat, "if you only walk long enough."

- Alice and the Cheshire Cat from *Alice In Wonderland*

It does help to have some structure for your thinking, envisioning, and documenting. So here are five key questions to guide you along that road:

1. What? You say you want to build something great, something lasting, something that you might be able to offer to your children, or your employees - or sell for an amount that represents a fitting return on your years of investment, labor, and leadership.

So what, exactly, do you want that to look like, be like, and feel like? Do you see it so clearly in your mind that you can describe it down to the details of the decor, your structure and operations, your gross revenue and your net profit?

2. Where? This is more than physical or geographic location though it includes that. Will you have one location, five, or twenty? Will it be strictly a brick-and-mortar operation or will you have a robust online presence, as well? Will your reach be local, regional, or state or nation-wide?

3. When? Do you see this being accomplished in three years or five? Or ten? Do you have an idea of what will need to be put into place first, then after that, then after that? At what point might you need to add employees? When will you hire your next one? Do you have managers yet? If not, when will that happen?

4. Why? This, my friend, is the most important and possibly the most difficult question to answer. You say you want to do all this, but WHY? What is your deep, heartfelt reason or purpose for pursuing this? Your "Why" will need to become the "why" of your employees, your managers, your team. *(Here's a hint: it's not money!)*

5. How? This question is usually the first one people ask themselves. But it needs to be the last one. It is counter-productive and really pointless to talk about how you will build something if you are not clear as to what you are building. (And why...) It is tantamount to saying, "I'm gonna build a house!" and then going to Home Depot, buying a boatload of materials, hauling it off to a lot somewhere and then trying to put it all together. Without plans.

Plan your work. Write it down. Work your plan.

Part 3 – People and Culture

It's About Relationship

No matter what spiffy marketing or sales terms we choose to use, the reality is that we are all engaged in "relationship building". Whether it is working to build a new relationship - finding and making a customer - or working to maintain an existing relationship - customer service, client fulfillment, doing what we do and doing it well - it is still all about relationships.

It is quite disconcerting to see and hear some of the terminology that is tossed about in a seemingly thoughtless manner when business owners and marketers speak of customers. The tendency is to become objective and impersonal when we think about finding new customers, or in "upselling" existing customers. And the danger is that we become mechanical and passionless in our dealings with these people and forget that we are dealing with, well, people.

People buy from people
I was reminded of this after receiving a great newsletter update from Chris Brogan's Human Business Works, a company that he founded. Its stated goal is to *"grow sustainable, relationship-minded businesses"* by offering personal development and business growth education and strategies.

What stands out for me in all of this is the phrase "relationship-minded businesses." In my book, all businesses should be "relationship-minded" - that is the essence of a business.

Or it should be.

If you are not relationship-minded as a business owner then you can only be relationship-*unminded*! Or perhaps we could say it this way: if your mind is not on relationships with your customers then you are essentially unrelationship-minded. Which is probably not a proper word. But it works here!

All businesses should be "relationship-minded"...
Finding, making and keeping great customers are based on relationships. When all is said and done, we do business with people,

not businesses. And when it comes to running and building a great business we can only accomplish that by building, cultivating, and fostering relationships with our customers, our employees, our vendors and suppliers, our investors, lenders, creditors - even our families and loved ones.

Without that there really is no business, no success, and no point.

Are We Having Fun Yet?

Is it possible to run and build a successful business and still have fun? Is it even important to *have* fun at work? I think it is. And I think it is necessary. And, in fact, I firmly believe that if you are not having some fun somewhere in your business then you are doing something wrong!

As an employee I want to be able to come to work for you and know that somewhere between the banality and menial tasks that all jobs possess, there is a spark of fun and lightness that I can look to in my days and in my weeks.

As the owner, it is your job to make that possible. Yes - you are not only the CEO - Chief Executive Officer - you are also the CFO - Chief FUN Officer. You can delegate much of what this role entails and you must foster and cultivate and encourage a culture and mindset of fun within the ranks.

We know it's not all play, but all work makes for a dull job and a dull company and a dull product or service.

What are you going to do to create some fun on the job?

Excellence Or Greatness?

☐　Excellent, *adj.* **1.** *Archaic.* Excelling; superior. **2.** Extremely good of its kind; first-class; hence, of great worth; eminently good.
☐　Excel, *v.* **1.** To go beyond or surpass in good qualities or deeds; to outdo. – *syn.* exceed.

This is not meant to be a scholarly or technical assessment of excellence and greatness. It is, however, an attempt to distinguish between the somewhat obsessive pursuit of excellence, so admirably addressed in Tom Peter's 1982 book *In Search of Excellence*

Another book which serves as a type of counterbalance to Peter's work is *Firms of Endearment.* Instead of pursuing excellence, this book's authors show how companies that strive to endear themselves to all their stakeholders can out-perform companies that are not stakeholder-focused in building shareholder wealth. Yet they both purport to explore avenues that businesses may take towards a goal of excellence. And their "definitions" of excellence differ markedly.

The thing about "excellence" is that is tied to a benchmark, a standard. It infers striving to outdo, to out-perform, and to attain a higher status or class. While there is certainly nothing inherently wrong with excelling, it does tend to become an end in itself. There is, in the essence of it, a sense of constantly striving, of "doing". It also tends to view the pursuit as a worthy strategy that may or may not lead to greater profitability, and does not necessarily attain to an enduring state of "greatness" - which brings us to *that* elusive quality...

☐　Greatness, *n.* **1.** The state, condition, or quality of being great; as, greatness of size, greatness of mind, power, etc. **2.** The property possessed by something or someone of outstanding importance or eminence.
☐　Great, *adj.***1.** Being much above the average in magnitude, intensity, importance, etc.; of person, their work, etc.; eminent; distinguished.

When it comes to businesses, it is a fair question to ask, as Bo Burlingham does in his book *Small Giants*, "What exactly is it that makes a company great?" His initial response to his own question was, "Of course, different individuals will come up with different answers, but I figured we could all benefit by considering the possibilities, by asking ourselves what we really want out of business, out of work, and out of life..."

So, while excellence can be seen as a critical ingredient in achieving greatness, there is far more involved in sustaining and fostering greatness for the long haul. And the exact nature of that greatness is contingent in large part on the vision and the mission, or purpose, of the company and the owners.

Greatness, like excellence, is inherent throughout a great company. It is part of the fabric, the culture, the DNA of a business that would embody greatness. And it is something that involves, in my estimation, a spirit of great *leadership* from whence all things emanate; a spirit of caring that infuses the *culture;* and a spirit of *service* that marks every function, every transaction, and every person.

You can choose to be excellent, but still not be great. Yet, if you strive to be great, you must pursue excellence. This is not a contradiction - it is, however, a decision you must make.

Choose wisely.

Passionate About Service

It may sound a bit strange to talk about passion when it comes to customer service.

Perhaps, but I believe that having a real interest in and passion for what one does cannot help but to infuse that activity with power. And this is particularly true when we speak of serving others. And that is what we do in a business – no matter what our role – we exist to serve the customer. For without a customer there is no business.

There is a very big assumption at work here on "being passionate" and it is that you like what you're doing. Oh, maybe not every detail of your job certainly. But it is assumed that you really enjoy your work and look forward to being there. It is assumed, as well, that you have a genuine interest in the nature of your company's service or product. If you didn't, you wouldn't be working there, right?

Okay, so I may be pushing this assumption a bit far, I know. But this begs a really crucial question that must be addressed: If you don't like what you do then why are you doing it? If you are an employee this is a critical point to consider.

If you are a business owner... then you especially need to think about this. It's been said before that no one cares about your business as much as you do. So it naturally follows that if YOU don't like your business then...

How Does Being Passionate Show Up?

Dave Ramsey said it this way:
"The secret ingredient to small business success is you. You are the energy, the ideas and the passion. You are the enthusiasm and the smile that greets the customers."

People respond to people. Customers have an experience each and every time they interact with and do business with you and your company. And to a large extent the quality and impact of that experience rests on you – how you show up, how you conduct yourself, and especially by how much energy and passion you display. In other words, if you truly enjoy what you are doing and you truly believe in your product or service, it will not only be seen, but it will be felt!

Another statement by Dave Ramsey speaks to this idea:
"Everybody wants to be successful in the job and makes lots of money, but personal happiness is just as important. If you wake up jazzed about what you're going to do every day, chances are you'll be successful and happy. But if you wake up dreading the day and your job, then I can almost guarantee you won't be financially successful or happy.

I am not speaking of a false or manufactured interest. We have all experienced this at one time or another. The forced greeting, the strained smile – the perfunctory responses that have somehow been imposed on otherwise unengaged and dispassionate employees.

And I am not advocating overbearing intensity either! It can a bit unnerving to be greeted by someone in a place of business who is overly forward, unnaturally animated, or in some way needlessly intense. What I am speaking to is authenticity. If you truly love your work and love what you offer or provide for people, then it will show.

Be real, be authentic.

And have fun!

Is There Anybody Out There?

Nothing is more distracting or dismaying to a customer than to feel ignored. While we may not say this aloud or even think it consciously, we as customers want to be the center and sole focus of the employee engaging us. It is terribly frustrating for a customer to have to wait for service. While that may not be a reasonable or fair frustration, it is a hallmark of our society – we want what we want now, if not sooner! And we want to be treated as if we were the only customer in the store.

As an employee, the challenge many times is to be continually focused and *present* - that is, mentally and emotionally and physically right there for the customer. Because you know that there are a multitude of other concerns, tasks or functions that are calling for your attention. If you find yourself having to multi-task while serving a customer you know this challenge. Yet, it remains paramount that when you are working with a customer either in person or even on the phone that he or she must be your single object of focus and concern.

Have you ever gone into a shop and the employee at the counter failed to acknowledge you? You glance over at them, wondering if they even know you walked in, and notice that they are busy with their cell phone.

You are not their focus right then. You're not even on their radar!

Don't be that employee.

You Must be Present to Win
Part of the secret of being present is in staying focused on *why* you do what you do. It is more than a job, more than taking care of customers, and more than simply making money. When all is said and done, the only reason a business exists is to make a customer. The customer, for good or bad, is the only reason you and I have a job!

This may seem obvious, but think about it: without a customer there really is no business. The truth is your job is to serve the customer above all else. That truly is "job number one". What you do in your particular role or position in your company is secondary to serving the customer. In fact, the customer is the only reason you do what you do in your position.

With that somewhat painfully obvious thought in mind I want to stress that the equally obvious – or what should be obvious – response of any employee is to be intentionally present with a customer. Always.

What does this look like? Paying attention. Actually listening. Intentionally ignoring distractions. Causing the customer to feel that – for the moments you two are engaged – that they are the only other person in the room.

You must live in the present, launch yourself on every wave, find your eternity in each moment." – Henry David Thoreau

How we spend our days is, of course, how we spend our lives. – Annie Dillard

Culture Matters

One of the most slippery and elusive concepts to articulate and define in your business is its culture.

Every company has one. It is the prevailing collective mindset and attitude of the staff. It is a reflection of the leadership. It colors and influences every aspect of the business.

And it exists by default, or by design.

In the words of Louis V. Gerstner, Jr. former CEO at IBM, "The thing I have learned at IBM is that culture is everything." That may seem a bit of an overstatement, an attempt at corporate hyperbole in order to underscore the importance of company culture. I believe he was right on the mark. In a business, culture IS everything.

So what is a business owner to do? For one, culture can be impacted, influenced and improved. And that task falls to the leader and, consequently, to the leadership team. A "bottom up" shift in a company's culture is unlikely and usually undesirable. It is the domain and the duty, if you will, of the leader in the business to shape and foster the culture of that business.

The only thing of real importance that leaders do is to create and manage culture. – Edgar Schein, Professor MIT Sloan School of Management

Robert Nardelli failed in his role as CEO of The Home Depot because he dismissed and disrespected the long established and positive culture that existed upon his arrival. It was the culture and the prevailing conceptions about who they were and what their mission was, that had made The Home Depot the giant that it had become. No corporate strategy could reverse the damage done to a culture that was reduced to dispirited and resentful employees, fearful of losing their jobs.

As a leader it is incumbent upon you to take a careful measure of your company's culture. It is your challenge to breathe fresh life into it, if necessary, and to invigorate it with a fresh sense of common purpose and the inspiration of a compelling vision.

Get to know your culture.

The Power Of Play

According to author Hara Estroff Marano in Psychology Today:
"It can truly be said that we are made for play; after all, humans are among the very few animals that play as adults. What the evidence adds up to is this: we are most human when we play—and just because we play.

Like art, play is that quintessential experience that is almost impossible to define—because it encompasses infinite variability—but which we all recognize when we see, or experience. So let us go back to the beach in an attempt to understand all that contributes to such a necessary, and exalted, psychological state.

The beach is, above all else, Somewhere Else, far enough away from home, office, and everyday routines in character and distance. That dislocation sets the stage for us to be attuned to the moment, to relax our focus on long-term goals. Being at the beach invariably forces a measure of spontaneity. We bring few of our usual possessions and tools. We are forced to recline, stretch out, relax."

It can also be said that there is power in play at work, in our business, in the way we interact and relate. Despite the fact that running and growing your business is indeed real serious stuff, it doesn't mean you have to always be serious. In the infamous words of the Joker, "Why so serious?"

There are parameters and a mutually understood sense of propriety in a healthy company culture that allows for and encourages play and playfulness. It is your job to communicate these and model them for your employees. The benefits are many: play can inspire you to think differently, it reduces stress, increase a sense of lightness, reduce struggle, conflict and worry, enhance energy levels, and - oddly enough - open you to opportunities to take risks.

According to life coach, Marianne St. Clair, "For too many of us, what is considered taking a risk is sometimes nothing more than taking an easier course. Play helps us release those thoughts that are locked in the head and the heart. Play also helps us learn our way, develop curiosity, learn to think, make new choices, discover special talents, build social relationships, make things less scary, and experience new enthusiasm for life."

So... go out and play! It'll do you good.

And have fun!

Greatness In Serving

"Be not afraid of greatness; some are born great, some achieve greatness, and others have greatness thrust upon them." - William Shakespeare

With all due respect to Mr. Shakespeare, I am of the persuasion that – for most of us – greatness is achieved. It is not that everyone does so. It is obvious that most people do not even strive for greatness. One might argue that there is a segment of the population that has no real desire to be "great". For them – and this includes business owners – merely being good is good enough.

My contention is that it really shouldn't be good enough to simply be good or acceptable. Becoming great at something, as an individual, as an organization – whatever it may be – is an aspiration that is both noble and ennobling. It is what we are wired for.

But greatness is not simply being "the best" or "being somebody". It is a state of being that inspires and enables others to greatness, as well.

"There is a great man who makes every man feel small. But the real great man is the man who makes every man feel great." - Gilbert Keith Chesterton

It also my contention that greatness dwells in and springs forth from a spirit of service and serving. There is nothing subservient or meek about having a servant's heart. Some of the strongest and most willful of men have been great servants. Greatness is a seeming paradox: to be truly great is to be a servant and in serving one will find true greatness.

"Everybody can be great... because anybody can serve. You don't have to have a college degree to serve. You don't have to make your subject and verb agree to serve. You only need a heart full of grace. A soul generated by love." - Martin Luther King Jr.

Thoughts On Culture

Company cultures are like country cultures. Never try to change one. Try, instead, to work with what you've got. – *Peter Drucker*

A culture of discipline is not a principle of business; it is a principle of greatness – *Jim Collins*

A company's culture is often buried so deeply inside rituals, assumptions, attitudes, and values that it becomes transparent to an organization's members only when, for some reason, it changes. – *Rob Goffee*

Real commitment is rare in today's organization … 90% of the time what passes for commitment is compliance. – *Peter Senge*

Culture is a framework in which we communicate – *Stephen Roberts*

The thing I have learned at IBM is that culture is everything. – *Louis V. Gerstner, Jr.*

Culture is a little like dropping an Alka- Seltzer into a glass - you don't see it, but somehow it does something – *Hans Magnus Enensberger*

The single biggest problem in communication is the illusion that it has taken place. – *George Bernard Shaw*

Simple, clear purpose and principles give rise to complex and intelligent behavior. Complex rules and regulations give rise to simple and stupid behavior. – *Dee Hock*

The way management treats their associates is exactly how the associates will then treat the customers. – *Sam Walton*

The Family Culture

"Ohana means family. Family means nobody gets left behind or forgotten." - Lilo Pelekai, *Lilo & Stitch*

There is a certain quality to family units that embodies caring and support. And there is a word used in Hawaii that captures this well. Part of Hawaiian culture, **'ohana** means family in an extended sense of the term, including blood-related, adoptive or intentional. It emphasizes that families are bound together and members must cooperate and remember one another. In actual Hawaiian culture, however, the term 'ohana is strictly used for blood relations.

Yet the word is often used in reference to friends and honored guests. Not to be taken literally, of course, but in spirit.

As a business, your culture determines in large part not only how employees care and support one another - or not - but how this is exemplified with your customers.

Or not.

'Ohana is also a spirit, an attitude, a mindset. In a bit of a more figurative sense it speaks of caring for others just as if they were family. As business owners we can get caught up in well-intentioned, but somewhat meaningless gestures and words about caring for customers, great service, and so on. But the danger is that they become just... words.

Infusing a spirit of 'ohana into your company's culture, however, requires forethought, intentionality, and effort. Not to mention exampleship.

Here's a question for you: Do you really care about your customers? Don't just react and say, "Of course!" - think about what all that implies. And do you really care for your employees? How does this show up in your business? What things do you say or do that expresses that care? Because if you don't care enough, neither will your employees.

And neither will your customers.

Mahalo!

Why Are We Doing This?

Every business venture begins with a Purpose. While there may be secondary or ancillary purposes such as making a living, being freed from a boss, a cubicle, whatever - there is always a primary, overriding Purpose that drives the decision to start and build a business.

It's just that sometimes that Purpose isn't always clear at the beginning.

Most businesses start with some vague notion of a plan, maybe even a thoughtful strategy, but more often than not it is simply full-steam ahead and work, work, work! But over time, as the rush of the start-up phase begins to die down a bit, the realization sets in that a Plan is needed so that the owner can hope to achieve something more than simply work, work, work.

And behind that Plan lurks their Purpose, perhaps vague and undefined, but there all the same.

The power of having formulated a Plan often stirs another rush of inspiration and energy. Goals and objectives become prizes to be taken, and challenges and setbacks become battles to be won. But as the months turn into years, the charge becomes a march, and the march becomes a marathon. Yet the Plan remains, the Purpose is still there, and Patience settles in.

And now, armed with experience and hindsight, the business owner often revisits the reasons why he or she decided to start this thing in the first place. And some - the fortunate or wise ones perhaps - rediscover that Purpose. And with the discovery they decide to bring clarity and depth to it and realize that they have a reason and a cause, something greater than simply growing a business, which ignites a deeper motivation and a brighter inspiration.

They have a Purpose.

With their newly defined Purpose the need for a well-thought out Plan becomes acutely apparent. And the experience and hindsight of the past years makes it very clear that Patience is required. The Plan, informed by their Purpose, is framed within the understanding of having Patience.

And now, with a Purpose, a Plan, and Patience, and Great Business is born.

The Importance Of Being Earnest

While this has nothing to do with the novel by Oscar Wilde, it does have everything to do with being both real and passionate.

Being real is the aspect of earnestness that is defined as "marked by or showing deep sincerity or seriousness". Your business - your product or service - may be good and, in fact, may be the best thing out there. But it is not perfect. Nothing is. And nothing goes perfectly every time. In other words, being real about you, your business, and what you do or offer means being sincere and serious in acknowledging limitations.

On the other side is the facet of earnestness that is marked by zeal. This is your passion, your enthusiasm, your sincerely driven sense that what you are and what you do really is good, really has great value, and really deserves a customer. These are what people respond to and resonate with in your attitude, your approach, your words - whether spoken or written.

Unbridled excitement or passion is not conducive to healthy enterprise. Being experienced as coming on too strong, or being overly enthusiastic about a product or service that doesn't merit all that much excitement - well, it may well repel prospects instead of attract them

On the other hand, deadly serious and unbearably grave may only work well for undertakers or wedding planners. (Yes, that was a joke) Blaise Pascal famously said that, "Earnestness is enthusiasm tempered by reason."

The ideal is a delicate balance that we know as earnestness - a really good word that doesn't get much use these days. And it IS important. Because unsullied earnestness conveys authenticity, transparency, and realness.

Be real. That's what *you* want, and that's what your customers want.

The Golden Rule

"Do unto others as you would have them do unto you." Great quote. Great principle. Too bad more businesses don't take it to heart. One does not have to be a Christian, or even particularly religious or spiritual, to appreciate the sublime power of that statement. If only we lived our lives consistently by this rule - the Golden Rule - how much nicer life on this planet would be...

As business owners we have the privilege and the opportunity to turn customer expectations on its head by implementing processes that work to guarantee that our customers are always treated as we would want to be treated. Is this unrealistic? I think not.

Two books, three actually, quickly come to mind as I ponder this prospect: *PEAK,* by Chip Conley, *Secret Service*, by John DiJulius, and *Firms of Endearment*, by Rajendra Sisodia, Jag Sheth, and David B. Wolfe. All of them make direct references to, or indirect inferences, to the Golden Rule. They profile dozens upon dozens of highly successful businesses that appear to have leveraged the power of "doing business with heart". I call it "business from the heart."

"There was never a person who did anything worth doing that did not receive more than he gave." - Henry Ward Beecher

Is Everybody Happy?
It doesn't begin and end with your customers either. No, in fact, it actually begins with your employees. Yes, them. There is an old saying that is probably not very PC, but it fits here: "When mama ain't happy, nobody's happy." In an analogous way this holds true for our businesses - if your staff isn't happy, nobody's happy. And if your customers aren't happy because the employees weren't happy then... well, you get the idea.

There are also the vendors and suppliers to consider. And, for some, investors and shareholders. And for all of us, there is our community, whether it is the local neighborhood that has so faithfully supported our business, or the community of Planet Earth. Having a business with heart does not stop at the cash register.

Got heart?
Your mission, should you decide to accept it, is to perform a diagnostic evaluation of your company's heart. First you might want to check for a pulse. But definitely make it a strategic endeavor to determine the extent to which you, your employees, and anyone else attached to your business, truly operate from a stance and a spirit of heartful service. Heart will trump technical excellence every time. Heart will outbid low prices every time. Heart will carry your business farther than any strategic business plan ever will.

Don't simply be a "business owner" - have heart!

Real Life

Sometimes, despite our best efforts, our personal life intrudes upon our business life.

We try to keep a handle on it, valiantly maintaining that separation between the office and the home, the business enterprise and the personal concerns. But it is difficult even in the best of times. When bad things happen, then what?

The truth is that business, once stripped of its branding adornments, signage, policies and procedures, and all the stuff that makes it a "business", is simply a collection of relationships between people. Customers, investors, suppliers, distributors, employees, and so forth - oh... and you, the owner. So there are all these relationships that work together in an orchestrated dance, if you will, and the end result each day is that we are "doing business".

And it is done by people. And people have issues and problems.

The Humanity of it All
So what do you, as an owner, do when one of your employees suffers a personal loss? Be it a divorce or the death of a loved one, a tragedy of that magnitude can and usually does render an employee somewhat unfit for carrying out their part of the dance. So what do you do?

Most employers are caring enough, and wise enough, to give that person space and time, and even some help of some sort. Because we're people after all. Fair enough.

But what happens when it is YOU?

What happens when you the owner, the boss, the CEO suffer a loss or tragedy of some sort? Do you stay home? Do you try to keep up the dance and worry about affecting your staff or customers with your inability to contain your hurt and grief? Some do. Actually, too many try to.

What about just being real?

These are the times that not only try a person's soul, they are the times that the relationships of that business can be strengthened and relied upon. It is a time when others can stretch themselves, step out of their "selves" and help. Because we're people after all.

Being Real
Someone once said that "life happens". And, unfortunately in many ways, it doesn't always happen well. And in those times, business - your business - is not the most important thing in the world. Nor should it be. Nor does anyone around you expect it to be.

So be real. And let the waves of bad times wash over your rigidly held separation for a bit.

It'll be alright eventually.

It's A Gift

Christmas is traditionally the time we give gifts, receive gifts, and really focus on the joy of giving. And this is as it should be, since for most folks that is the spirit of Christmas. But the shadow of it all is that too many of us tend to reserve the bulk of our giving for the holidays and maybe some birthdays here and there.

Giving is often not a part of our culture.
It may be a part of your personal make-up, to be sure, but is it truly an integral part of your business environment and company culture? Is it a quality and a mindset that you intentionally foster and impart to your employees and your company's "community"? It should be!

One of the key aspects of a truly great company is caring. When people know that you care - "you" being you as the owner, you as a company, and you as a brand - then they care more about what you have to say and have to offer. And we can show how much we genuinely care about others, about quality, about greatness, when we give.

There are many ways to "give".
Giving can show up as tangible items - samples, discounts, giveaways, information, etc. For employees it can be any number of perks including bonuses, paid days off, seminar training underwritten by the company, and so on.

But giving can also show up as time, effort, concern, mentoring, and even friendship. It shows up as a natural and almost spontaneous way of being and doing, as well as an intentional and planned approach to functioning and doing business.

Here are three ways for building a culture of giving:

1. Be a role model
As in any other facet of your business, it all starts with the Leader. It may sound simplistic, but here the operational truth is that people "hear" what you do much better than what you say. Be the initiator

and the perpetuator of giving in your company. And as you set the stage and the example, others will step on board.

2. Create "planned" giving activities

Spontaneity is crucial, but there is a place for intentional and premeditated giving. Strategically planned and scheduled actions, events, etc. designed to exemplify the spirit of caring by giving is critical for forming the scaffolding that supports an environment for spontaneous giving.

3. Actively look for new ways to give

Nothing says "I don't really care." more than a perfunctory gift. And the problem with giving is that it can devolve from being an intentional lifestyle and culture choice, to a mechanical and empty pattern of gestures. So actively seeking out or creating variety and novelty in your giving keeps you and your staff authentic and "real" in their ongoing efforts to foster a culture of giving.

So have a wonderful Christmas - and think about what you are going to give someone next week!

Gimme Structure

Everyone wants structure.

I know - they might complain about it, balk at it, and even claim that it is unnecessary or confining - but the truth is that we all need and thrive with structure.

So why are your employees so unclear as to what they are supposed to be doing every day? And how, exactly, they are supposed to be doing it? And what the standards are around what they are supposed to be doing?

And even *why* they do it?

"Just the facts, ma'am."
Granted, your employees probably do know what they are supposed to do - and how - for the most part. But the fact is that in too many companies the lines are fuzzy, the expectations are vague, and the standards are confused or non-existent.

And this causes problems. But you already know that, don't you?

"But I've told them a dozen times already!" you say. Yes, and still you find yourself answering the same questions, fielding the same performance issues, fighting the same fires. Trying to build and manage a "lean, well-oiled machine" feels more like herding cats.

Every day.

There is an easier and better way. And it doesn't require an MBA or rocket science. No, in fact, it requires nothing more complicated than a clearly written, documented description of the responsibilities, expectations, and standards for each and every position in your organization.

And a process for communicating this document to each person occupying a position in your organization, clearly, concisely, and regularly.

Talk to me!
While this approach is, on its face, simply a structured method for establishing and documenting the tasks for each position - think of them as "job descriptions on steroids" - it is really an extension of the main task of every business leader: communication.

At the risk of oversimplification it can be said that what lies at the heart of most every business problem, dysfunction or failure is a lack of effective communication. And the leader (and the leader's managers) must make effective communication their primary function and responsibility.

If you tell me what I am responsible for in my job, show it to me in writing, support it with clear expectations and standards, and periodically reinforce this on a regular basis, then I can be held accountable for fulfilling those responsibilities.

Not just a "job description"
At EMyth the process and the resulting document was often referred to as a Position Agreement. While you can call it whatever feels best for your organization, the process is straightforward and structured in such a way as to involve your employees directly.

Documenting the tasks and requirements for all of your company's positions is serious business, not just paperwork. They are the tangible expression of a company's philosophy; a way of doing business. They embody the spirit of how people throughout an organization can work together to achieve their accountabilities and experience success individually and as a team.

So get out there and start communicating!

How Hard Can It Be?

I just spent a week in Arizona last month.

Arizona in January is not that bad. But, in Prescott Valley, where we stayed, it IS freaking cold! So the occasional rain showers turned to snow.

Oh, and in addition to 7 nights in three different hotels, we ate out for every meal. This brings me to an occupational hazard of mine.

As a business owner do you ever find yourself critiquing and analyzing other business's operations, processes and **customer service**? (Or lack of it!) Well, that's what I caught myself doing throughout the entire week. And I couldn't help myself.

While my observations were by no means scientific or structured, the perceptions, impressions, and experiences I gathered gave me a very distinct if anecdotal conclusion: far too many businesses suffer from dysfunctional operations, ineffective (or simply non-existent) processes, and customer service that consistently falls in the 3 out of 5 star range.

Is that the best we can do?

Now, I know that this is not a fair representation of small businesses as a whole, but I bet it is pretty close to the real picture. We have all heard cries of lousy customer service in American stores and businesses. We all know that our own businesses, as well as our neighbor's, are sorely lacking in many fundamental and essential **processes**.

In other words, despite any number of stellar companies there are across the small business landscape, the truth is that most fall short of what they could be.

And should be.

I am a firm believer that greatness - or at least the potential for it - resides within every individual. This is what I strive to tap into and engage with in my business coaching - the often latent greatness that is stirring with the heart and mind of my business owner client. Imagine that, much like your computer with the ubiquitous label that reads "Intel Inside", you have a virtual label across your heart that reads "Greatness Inside".

And because the key factor in building a truly great company is great leadership, there is hope for every business owner in building a great business, a company that consistently ranks in the 5 star range of effective operations and remarkable customer service.

So, what has your own research shown you?

Part 4 – Other Stuff

Promote Or Die

pro·mote

1. to help or encourage to exist or flourish; further: *to promote world peace.*

2. to encourage the sales, acceptance, etc., of (a product), esp. throug h advertising or other publicity.

I kind of like the idea of helping or encouraging to exist or flourish - which is why this post is entitled "Promote or Die!" We must be continuously helping and encouraging the existence and flourishing of our businesses. It is truly a never-ending process.

The second definition, of course, is what most of us with a business think of when we hear or use the terms "promote" or "promotion". Not that this has to be done strictly with advertising or special sales, etc. No, in fact, when I use the word here I am thinking of promoting in the broader and much more inclusive sense: anything and everything we do to increase and maintain awareness of our business, our products, and our services.

An expense or an investment?

The problem is that far too many business owners think and act as if promotion must **a.)** cost money, and **b.)** consist of advertising or paid publicity of some sort. This is not only short-sighted it is dangerous since these kinds of tactics are not available to most small business owners on a regular basis.

And every day that you are not promoting your business is a day that you are losing potential customers. So what is an owner to do?

Thinking beyond the known and the obvious is a start. Recognizing that anything which gets your business in front of prospective customer's mind is legitimately considered promotion. Word of mouth, referrals, signage, direct mail, press releases, business cards, people in costumes, feature stories, articles, Little League sponsorships, community efforts, donating of services, floats in a city parade, open houses, elementary school field trips... and so much more. Low cost or no cost, the possibilities are almost endless and the potential is truly unlimited.

Random acts of promotion are fine, but a well thought-out strategy and a promotion plan is better. The key, of course, is to simply *do something!*

Are You Branded?

We have heard plenty over the years regarding brands, branding, being branded, the need for you and I to be branded... and it never ends really. So my question is this: what, exactly, constitutes a "brand"?

Seth Godin once offered this definition: *"A brand is the set of expectations, memories, stories and relationships that, taken together, account for a consumer's decision to choose one product or service over another. If the consumer (whether it's a business, a buyer, a voter or a donor) doesn't pay a premium, make a selection or spread the word, then no brand value exists for that consumer."*

What struck me in his definition is the emphasis on the consumer - the customer - not the business or business owner, which is quite proper.

Let's turn to the sage Mad Man David Ogilvy: *"The intangible sum of a product's attributes: its name, packaging, and price, its history, its reputation, and the way it's advertised."* Now there is something for the business and the customer to contribute. And I agree that brand, however you define it, is both intangible yet consists of tangibles; it is ethereal yet substantial; and it is slippery and sticky.

Doesn't help much, does it?

If you are the "face" of your business, if your company's positioning and market perception are tied directly to you as a real person, then your brand is *you* for the most part. Yet even that is not the whole story. Your brand is everything you attempt to make it in the minds of your customers and prospects, and it is everything they hear, see, feel, experience and remember about you and your service.

And here is the big downside of "you-as-the-brand": if you leave or try to replace yourself then your "brand" and your brand equity go with you. There will be the ghost of a brand for a while - until your audience has forgotten you.

A company or product brand is a different animal altogether, however. It stays with the business or product with or without you, the owner. And despite the contingent of marketing gurus who pooh-pooh the emphasis on branding it is still critical, necessary, and - I would contend - unavoidable.

Brand happens. Put up a website, open a store, set up your roadside stand - branding has begun. How you dress it, what you say with it, how it performs, what it costs, the good, the bad, the ugly - it all swirls together into that ever-growing and ever-deepening enigma we call a "brand". So the importance and value of brand-building and brand management cannot be overstated.

What is your brand? Is it what you think it is? Has it grown by design? Or by default?

Feels like Business

"What comes from the heart, goes to the heart" - Samuel Taylor Coleridge

Too often, as business leaders, we tend to lose sight of the intangible - the truly important and valuable - as we focus on the immediate and the seemingly important tasks and issues that face us each day. It's not that these things don't need to be attended to - they do - but we run the risk of drifting into a default mode of "doing business" mechanically and without feeling.

And, you may ask, what's feeling got to do with it? Let me explain what I mean by "feeling" first. I'm referring to a state of awareness and intention first and foremost. A way of functioning in which you are always attentive to what you are doing and why. This is coupled with an undercurrent of intentionality - everything is being done or said with an immediate purpose or goal, and it is all working together synergistically towards the higher and long-range goal or objective.

In practice it means being attuned to others in your business interactions and their needs, intentions, and reactions. This includes all of your colleagues, peers, employees, customers, vendors or suppliers - everyone with which you interact on any level. It means transcending the mechanical functioning that often makes up the bulk of working life and moving in the realm of relational awareness.

Because at its heart business is nothing more than a collection of relationships: the buildings, the products or services, the incorporation papers, the marketing collateral - all of this is simply the tangible accoutrements that reflect a mental construct we call a "business".

Without the myriad of personal relationships the business is simply a fiction. A game that no one is playing.

And relationships require "feeling".

W I I FM – Is It On Your Dial?

There is the real question that every customer asks. Whether they realize it or not. Whether they vocalize it or not.

"What's in it for me?"

"How will this decision, this purchase, this service or product benefit me? Serve me? Make me happier?" As business owners we do well to remember that at all times and in every situation. As "marketers" for our businesses we must keep this reality in our focus as we develop marketing strategies and tactics. As "customer service reps" for our businesses we need to hold this reality before us day in and day out, despite the needs of the business or the unreasonableness of the customer.

Now this may seem unfair and even a bit patronizing.

Yet it is a reality of human nature and the very nature of commercial transactions: I trade you something you want for something I want. I give you two dollars - which allows you to pay your staff and eke out a bit of profit - and I get a gourmet cup of coffee - which makes me feel good and gives me a boost that I want or need. I win, you win.

But when you advertise your coffee shop and I see your ad or your sign, my first subconscious reaction is something along the lines of "How will that benefit me?" or "What's in it for me?" While I realize that this is not a new revelation nor does it rise to the level of quantum physics, it is almost always forgotten, overlooked, dismissed, or misunderstood.

Be prepared to answer that question in a compelling and remarkable way and you will be planting seeds for a great business.

ABP (Always Be Promoting!)

Promotion! One of the most pressing accountabilities that fall upon the business owner-as-marketer is the never-ending need to promote his or her business. Advertising alone will not suffice. Publicity and word of mouth are great, but they are not enough. Even the seemingly ubiquitous scope and reach of the Internet and social media won't keep the name out there.

Attention spans are notoriously short and stimulus comes at us so relentlessly that any message we saw or heard a week ago is already in danger of being deleted from the mental files and soon forgotten. So the owner must continuously and persistently promote.

Fortunately, this has become easier than ever while the multitude of channels and media available can threaten to overwhelm the DIY marketer. Suffice it to say that not every new medium or device that comes into existence must be leveraged for non-stop promotion. In fact, sometimes the old maxim that "less is more" can serve us well in this arena. Strategy, planning, and sober-minded discrimination are needed here.

The temptation, too, is to just keep throwing spaghetti against the wall to see what sticks - especially when so much is free to use! But there is still only a limited batch of spaghetti any one business owner has - and this approach will result in diluted, mis-applied, and random lead generation and promotion efforts that result in little, if any, real awareness or real customers.

It is unfortunate, but often true that most small business owners, having to be their own marketing department, balk at research, tracking and quantification. "Who has time for that?" they ask. "I can't afford it." they will say. The sad truth is, however, that they cannot afford to NOT do it.

Research the options, determine a strategy, develop a plan, implement it, and continue it in.

Spread the word - and never let up!

Card Magic

A small, but potentially powerful tool is at your disposal.

It is "old school", low-tech, and incredibly affordable. Its versatility has yet to be diminished or fully leveraged. It was ubiquitous, but now is beginning to show signs of scarcity. Behold, the humble business card.

What started as a hybrid of a calling card and a trade card - depending on whose history you read - became the standard tool of early "social media". While these cards are still designed and printed by the tens of millions it seems that the dawning of the digital age has also brought the waning of the ephemeral age. Or not.

I still subscribe to the belief that tactile connections hold tremendous power and nothing compares to the sight and feel of a finely crafted, well printed business card. And, more importantly, nothing else can be so portable while so visible and hold such tremendous potential for variety and novelty.

Cards can be made to say anything you want, in as many variations as you want, and cost relatively pennies to produce. The advent of digital printing and Print On Demand services have rendered the field of business card printing relatively a loss leader for most businesses. While this may a bit of bad luck for printers it is a boon to entrepreneurs! With some innovative thinking and creative imagination just about anything is possible.

I challenge you to take a fresh look at your business cards - assuming you bothered to get any - and imagine what they *could* look like. Imagine what new ways you could get them into the hands of prospects. Imagine how much fun it could be to produce and distribute a variety of cards in various sizes and styles, for a variety of purposes, for a variety of prospects.

Imagine!

Making Dents

There are many things we can give our lives to: causes, crusades, loved ones, intellectual pursuits... many things that can consume our time, our energies, and our passions. Some of these are noble and worthwhile. Others are trivial and insubstantial. But building a great enterprise, a business that can stand on its own and continue long after we are gone - this is the stuff of legacies.

The passing of Steve Jobs triggered a great outpouring of philosophizing and punditry over the legacy he created and left in his wake. It was Jobs who made the statement at one time that he wanted to "make a dent in the Universe." Now that's a dream worth pursuing! So the question I pose here is what is the legacy you are creating? What is the impact you want to have on your world and those around you?

"If you have built castles in the air, your work need not be lost; that is where they should be. Now put the foundations under them."

It was these words of Henry David Thoreau first stirred me to dream large. And more importantly, to understand and believe that dreaming was acceptable and not the mark of a flighty and undependable mind. I came to realize that without the dream a vision could not be truly born.

And without the vision there can be no great undertaking or enterprise, no driving passion to build and achieve, no lasting legacy to be had.
A dream alone is no guarantee of success. But a dream, a castle in the air, cannot become real if you do not work to build the foundation it needs to stand.

So go ahead and dream. Build your castle amongst the clouds. And in the morning begin laying the stones for the foundation.
And never look back.

Promises, Promises

"Customer service is not a department."
"Every employee is a customer service rep."
"Your call is valuable to us."
"I'll pay you back when I get my next paycheck."
"I'll still love you in the morning."

Broken promises come in all shapes, sizes and flavors. But the promise of service in a business is more than something that is routinely broken and ignored - it is a breach of trust. For business owners it must be - absolutely has to be - a given: service, great service, exceptional service, is and always will be what we provide. Period.

Every aspect of our business functions and operations should be designed with this end in mind.

Service to and for our customers is never - never! - to be viewed as a value-added benefit or option. It is never an add-on or accessory.

Service is never an option.

It's More Than A Transaction

Think about your business. If you are a business owner, think about the lives you touch with your business. If you are an employee in a business, think about the lives you impact. Every workday, every week, every month – year after year. By design or by default you have a real influence on untold numbers of people simply through the act of carrying out a business.

Businesses large and small possess the potential to have a dynamic and influential impact and influence on their customers, their community, their industry… the world. (*Apple comes to mind!*)

What impact do you want to have? How do you want to influence your world?

My point here is that because you are orchestrating a complex web of relationships we call a business you therefore have the power to choose the type of impact and influence you would like to have on all these constituencies – these customers, employees, vendors, suppliers, investors, friends and family of these customers, employees, etc.

As Peter Parker's uncle says in the movie Spiderman, *"With great power comes great responsibility*

Your business can serve as a platform and a well spring for good. It's up to you what that will look like, but the fact is you do influence the people you relate to in the course of running your business. The potential for shaping and affecting the lives of hundreds or even thousands – even if in a relatively small way – is incredibly vast.

And, yet, it can be sabotaged.

Really.

By poor service. By an average, unexceptional customer experience. By being a business that doesn't care.

Don't be that business.

Know Me, Like Me, Trust Me. Please.

I don't spend too much space discussing sales or actual marketing on this site. However, it occurred to me recently that if we are to focus our efforts and energies on creating a great business, then the larger purpose has to be so we can make great customers.

And the finding, getting and keeping of customers is what marketing - and sales - is all about.

It is quite easy to become overwhelmed and mentally numbed by all the reams of content and talk, talk, talk about marketing one finds on the Internet. And that, perhaps unfortunately, is where many of us spend a great deal of our time. And the marketing talk almost always leans to the "latest" and "best" methods, tactics, approaches, and strategies.

What is a business-owner-as-marketer to do?!

Step back. Breath deep. And think about what your instinct tells you really works. Getting people who need what you got, to know you, to like you, and to trust you. Simple enough... but it's the "getting" that often stumps us, isn't it?

Allow me to reintroduce a tried and true (some might say trite) concept: the funnel. Actually, I prefer the imagery of a spider's web, but there are some morbid connotations to that for some people. So we'll use the venerable funnel illustration instead.

Gotta Have Business to Have a Business
Imagine the wide end of the funnel representing your reach within your marketplace. The narrow end of the funnel is where you are - product or service in hand - waiting to surprise and delight your newly acquired customers. Along the length of the funnel imagine various tactics, tools, medium, etc. that work to draw a prospective customer further into the funnel until they arrive at your door (or website, book cause, etc.). When all is said and done, this is still the primary means for creating customers.

The question then is this: what great things are you doing to get people to know you? What great things are you giving them so that they can come to like you? And what great things are you doing for them so that they learn to trust you? Greatness works both directions - internally with you, your staff, your product or service - and externally towards your prospects, your customers, your vendors, your investors, your community.

By the way - in case you are wondering - word of mouth and referrals are still far and away the most effective, the most authentic, and the most cost-effective means of filling the funnel.

So keep marketing. And keep being great!

PERMISSION TO BE GREAT

"So you want to strive for greatness. Who told you that you could do that? I mean, who do you think you are anyway?"

"Face it – you're not much of an entrepreneur. Heck! You can barely call yourself a business owner without feeling like a phony."

"The fact is, you're just... what? A shopkeeper. A mere manager!

"Get real!"

Know that voice? The one in your head? The one that constantly whispers - sometimes shouts - that you can't do it, be it, create it?

Yeah. *That* voice.

I'm here to tell you to stop listening to it. Why? Because it is an immutable fact that you are imbued with greatness and that it can come *from* you and *into* whatever you desire to achieve and build.

I once heard a business owner/

Bottom line: you can DO this!

I had an image come to mind recently (a bit of an epiphany if you will indulge me) of a badge pinned right above our hearts, engraved with the words: "Greatness Inside."

So stop listening to that lying voice in your head. And give yourself permission to step into the greatness that you truly possess. And infuse that greatness into your business, your company culture, your employees... your world.

I'd like You To Meet My Business

If your company were an actual person what would they be like? What kind of personality traits and characteristics would be evident? Who, exactly, is that person?

While this can an enlightening and even fun exercise, at the end of the day we all realize that a business is not a person (even if it is a one person business!) A business is an entity composed of any number of people, and the "personality" of that business is, in part, an amalgam of all those disparate personalities. Yet, to a customer or client, that business still projects a personality of sorts.

So the question is this: As a business, are you who you say you are? And even more importantly, are you who you think you are?

The term "brand" has been terribly abused, misused, and even over-used in the business and marketing world. But it is a valid and significant word, nonetheless. Your brand is your business. Your business is your brand. They are one and the same.

And your brand has two faces: the one you present either by design or default, and the one your customers see and experience.

So the challenge for you is to determine who you are as a business or, perhaps, who you want to be, and infusing that "personality" into every facet of your business and operations. It should live and breathe the brand, the values, and the purpose that you bring into it. In a very real way your business should be an expression of the best of you.

You Need A Story

Ok, so I fudged a bit with the title - you already have a story. Seriously.

If you have been paying attention over the last few years or so you will have noted a trend in advertising and marketing in general around this idea of a "story". Insurance companies trotting out real customers telling their story; multitudes of companies creating videos that portray their story; somewhat vague TV commercials with people most of us don't know, talking to us about their story as if they *are* someone we were supposed to know...

I think you get the idea.

Tell Me A Story
But here's the thing: stories still have power. They still possess the ability to get attention, appeal to our emotions, and draw us into themselves - even if we would not be interested otherwise. Listening to stories, telling stories, relating to stories - it's hardwired in us - it's in our DNA.

And your business really does have a story. And I am not referring to the history of your company and how it started. Yeah, that's a story, but not necessarily one your customers and prospects care to hear. No, there is a story that exemplifies and embodies who and what you are as a company. You have a story that is compelling, endearing, and impactful. Ok - maybe not a Pulitzer Prize story, but a good story all the same.

A really good company story is more like an anecdotal tale, one that illustrates the essence of your business at its best. It is what makes you and your business different and special.

Start With Why
But before you start scribbling away on your first draft of a company story, it will serve us to determine WHY, exactly, do you need your story communicated? Here are three reasons:

It is a compelling description of the "big idea" behind your company, the inspiration behind your business.

It gives you another tool to rally your employees and to attract the best recruits.

It gives you words to differentiate yourself from the rest.

But What Do I Say?
Think about this: What are your guiding principles? What matters to you most? What do you want in your business and your life to become genuine? How can you best illustrate that spirit? Think back through the years and find one incident, one anecdote that reflects the spirit. What can you say about its birth? Its energy? What fired your imagination? What is the cause, idea or spirit that you want your company and your employees to champion?

That is your story.

And your story can be a rallying cry for you and your employees. Once you have written it, share it with them. Your story should say, *"This is how we do it here when we are at our absolute best."* Inspire others to become part of the story. Use it to get people excited, to foster support, to recruit, to sell, and to impact your world in a way that matters.

So what's your story?

What's Your Brand Message?

Great question – and one that has a simple, but involved answer. Brand messaging, consistent communications, and an authentic voice does not come about organically. It must be the result of *Intention* and *Attention*.

Intention

As is true with anything in business that is important to the overall operation and success of that business, communication and the use of words must be part of your strategic purpose. A brand strategy working within the context of your intentional vision and shaped by your stated values and purpose – these are the drivers for your intentional communications strategy.

This can take the form of branding guidelines, communication policies, and the documenting of the company vision, values, and purpose. In addition, the message and voice that you want to be present and consistent throughout your organization must be modeled by yourself and your management team.

However, structured and strategic intentionality does not have to be complicated or onerous. The important thing is to know yourself first and foremost so that you can effectively communicate the essence of your vision and values to everyone in your organization. And whatever written support you feel can provide understanding should be created.

Attention

Another word for this might be "awareness". The idea is that you should always be fully conscious and aware of what you are doing, why you are doing it, and what is happening around that and because of what you are doing. And this includes what you say or write.

On the face of it, being aware may seem quite intuitive and simple. But human nature is such that our default mode is to slip into rhythms, routines, and ruts. What starts out as highly intentional and focused can, over time, devolve into functions of habit, mindless phrases, and meaningless words.

Attention requires a conscious and intentional effort. The purpose of striving to maintain both intention and attention is to achieve focus. Much has been written about the power of focus and it is easily seen demonstrated in life. World class athletes have developed the ability to harness intense focus which works to help them achieve their goals. It can be seen with artists, performers, writers, and even at work.

At times, this is experienced as what has become known as "flow", a concept proposed by Mihály Csíkszentmihályi. Imagine a broader, corporate version of this state operating in your business life – a state of collective "flow" where everyone is conscious of what they do and say, and why. This is roughly analogous to attaining a company-wide state of Intention and Attention. And the result is a corporate focus that helps everyone to achieve the highest aspirations of the company.

Your company's words matter. How do you make them count?

Words Matter

"Remember, then, that words are the only tools you will be given. Learn to use them with originality and care. Value them for their strength and their diversity. And also remember that somebody out there is listening." - William Zinsser, *On Writing Well*

We are animals of a unique order in that we, alone among all creatures, use language consisting of words to communicate. While it is understood that communication, even among humans, can occur with gestures, facial expressions, and non-word sounds, the fact is that even these actions are perceived in the form of words – unspoken and purely within our minds, but in words nonetheless.

So it is with us and always has been since the beginning of recorded history (which used words to make the record!)

In the seminal book, *On Writing Well*, William Zinsser was speaking to those who would desire to write – or were required to – when he made the statement that "words are the only tools you will be given." It is true for all facets of communication – regardless of the channel, the medium, or the format – we must use words to get our message understood. And in business it is not only important, but absolutely essential that we use words to their greatest effect.

Words: The Basis of All Communication

It is an interesting phenomenon that what we are most accustomed to we tend to be unaware of. Like air: no one thinks much of it until it is suddenly missing. Then it matters. But the fact is that it always mattered! But because it is so ubiquitous and ever-present we often fail to acknowledge it or be aware of it.

Words become the same thing for us. They are an invisible, ever-present commodity that we operate with unthinkingly for the most part. We think in words, we speak in words, words written, spoken, or in our minds are all around us and inside of us!

And the primary – if not exclusive – means with which we communicate to one another is through the medium of words.

Say What?

When words are unclear, misused, or in a form or language we do not understand, then communication suffers or ceases altogether. Even when we think we understand there is always the potential for some loss or lack of real communication. Anyone who has, or is, in an intimate relationship will have experienced those moments.

In life it is often a challenge to understand others and to be understood. In business it is vital that communication always be clear and easily understood. And yet this isn't always the case. Too often, real communication suffers for any number of reasons – and they all involve the use of words.

And this happens both internally and outwardly.

How well are you using your words?

The Nobility Of Work

I have been reading about one of my favorite people over the last few days, Abraham Lincoln. The book, Lincoln Unbound by Rich Lowry, brings forth some of the personal values and principles that guided the young Abe Lincoln and grounded him as an older man as he led the nation through its most wrenching crisis.

Some of these came vividly to light in the words he penned to a young man desiring to study law with him: *"Always bear in mind that your own resolution to succeed is more important than any other thing."*

At another point, writing to his law partner William Herndon, he expressed his philosophy for dealing with opposition and perceived setbacks:
"The way for a young man to rise, is to improve himself every way he can, never suspecting that anybody wishes to hinder him. Allow me to assure you, that suspicion and jealousy never did help any man in any situation. There may sometimes be ungenerous attempts to keep a you man down; and they will succeed, too, if he allows his mind to be diverted from its true channel to brood over the attempted injury... You cannot fail in any laudable object, unless you allow your mind to be improperly directed."

Lincoln held fast to the doctrine of hard work, thrift, generosity, and fair play. While many today might dismiss him as simply being a man of his time and irrelevant for today's culture, I contend that there are some values and principles that are timeless and perennially relevant. Human nature doesn't really change, despite our contemporary bias to the contrary.

As Lincoln put it to an aspiring lawyer almost 200 years ago, *"Work, work, work, is the main thing."* And this reality still holds for us today: anything worth having, worth building, worth achieving takes work. No amount of technology, "get-rich-quick" efforts, or positive thinking will replace the need for good, old-fashioned WORK!

The are multiple benefits of work beyond simply getting a thing done. But nothing can get done without work.

How's your work ethic today?

Practicing Essentials

I just had another great discussion with one of my coaching clients yesterday. Two, in fact. Two clients - completely different businesses and at different stages of business life - and almost the same discussion: How to get stuff done effectively?

After some questioning and a little digging it was quite apparent that neither of them had mastered the skills of personal time management and self-organization. And really, beyond the avoidance of some tasks and the undeniable reality of constant interruptions or unanticipated demands on their time, both clients agreed that even without these factors they were lacking in those essential leadership skills.

Keeping Up the Habit

Maybe "lacking" is the wrong word - more like "not practicing" them. They had allowed themselves to slip out of the habit of planning their days, capturing and maximizing their available time, getting and staying highly organized and, therefore, focused.

And it takes work! Most people, I have come to believe, are not naturally inclined towards these habits. It is not intuitive for most of us to think of our time in terms of budgeting and investing. It is not wholly natural for many of us to be well organized, structured in our work flow, and achieving clarity and focus in our tasks. But it can be done.

Both of these clients, having "fallen off the wagon" so to speak, pledged to go to work on improving - or resurrecting - their time management practices and to go back to their work areas with the goal of becoming more organized. They expressed an agreement that the two practices go hand-in-hand and that is difficult to be successful in one without practicing the other. It's hard to get and stay organized if you are not in control of your time, and it is challenging to plan and maximize your time each day if you are disorganized and unfocused.

Why Thinking About it Ain't Enough

I offer a simple variation on an age-old maxim:
"Plan your work, WRITE IT DOWN, and work your plan."

Too often the tendency is to plan our day mentally. Can I just say it won't work? It won't work. You might pull it off for a day, maybe two. But our brains our fickle and prone to lapses, leaks, and little glitches. The better path is to write out a daily and weekly plan. Monthly, too, is helpful.

And this approach is absolutely essential when it comes to accomplishing tasks, projects, and initiatives that span multiple days or involve multiple steps, etc. It is not enough to simply "plan" your work mentally - you gotta write it down!

Plan, Write, Work - we are pretty good with the planning: its effective execution that often escapes us. I will continue with this theme on Friday with an emphasis on the "Write" aspect. In the meantime, I would love to hear what your own "best practices" are around time management and self-organization.

Let the Games Begin

We don't necessarily associate being a business owner with a "game". Although we have *The Great Game of Business* by Jack Stack, it does seem a bit frivolous to talk about what we go through as being a game. In fact, Michael E. Gerber, in his book *The E-Myth Revisited*, used the concept of "a game worth playing" in reference to cultivating a culture of team members - and many people took exception at his choice of words.

Some folks are just allusion-challenged, I think. The concept of a "game" in reference to owning and running a business is usually meant to be allegorical. And there are many aspects of starting and building an enterprise that are similar to a sports game. We talk in terms of "the competition" and having "a team". Tracking sales and profitability is a way of "keeping score ". Managers are admonished to keep their "eyes on the ball".

And while the perceived goal or objective of starting a business is to build something that can be sold or handed down as a legacy, there is something inherent in the process apart from this that appeals to many entrepreneurs. Something that transcends the goals, the objectives, the 5-Year plans... there is *a love of the game*.

They may not use those terms or think of it in that frame, but there is a thrill and a fire that thrives on the work of building and "perfecting" their business. Something about the daily interactions with customers, vendors, or employees that excites and gratifies them deeply - far more deeply than profit margins or financial reward. There is something intrinsic in the act that keeps them going at it even if there IS no financial reward at times!

They do it for the love of the game.

So, why do you do it?

Motivated Or Inspired?

Sometimes inspiration comes from a place of need or want. And please note that I am speaking of "inspiration", not "motivation". We all know that motivation can come from the offer of great reward (positive) or from fear or dread (negative). A man being chased by an angry bear is no doubt highly motivated to run and to run as quickly as he can. Someone with an opportunity to make $1,000 for a few hours work can be equally motivated.

But inspiration is of a different nature. The word itself comes from the idea of something breathed into one's spirit, or divine guidance. To be inspired does not necessarily equate with being motivated, however. Yet, paradoxically, being greatly inspired can birth great motivation.

And this is what we often need.

Motivated to Inspiration
Consider Ulysses S. Grant. He was the top general of the Union forces during the Civil War, and eventually served two terms as President of the United States. And while he was considered a hero and venerated greatly by his contemporaries, he was not much of a business man. In fact, his only real success came as a soldier and somewhat as the Chief Executive. But in civilian life he did not prosper.

After leaving the White House, his lack of success at civilian life continued. He was a partner in a financial firm only to have his partner, Ferdinand Ward, embezzled their investors' money. Consequently, the firm went bankrupt in 1884, as did Grant. That same year, Grant learned that he was suffering from throat cancer. While his military pension was reinstated, he found himself and his family strapped for cash.

At the urging of his friends Grant began selling magazine pieces about his life, though he resisted the call to pen an autobiography. But the need for funds persisted. It was at this juncture that inspiration came in the form of the famed novelist Mark Twain.

Twain - also known as Samuel Clemens - had recently established a publishing company and needed a sure-fire bestseller to launch this enterprise. That need, coupled with a genuine desire to help his friend Ulysses S. Grant, pushed him to convince Grant to publish his memoirs.

Grant, realizing he was dying and that he had little to leave his family, negotiated a contract with Twain. The throat cancer began to rapidly do its damage and Grant found himself in a veritable life-or-death race to finish his memoirs and thus leave a legacy for his wife and children. He was wholly inspired and took to the task readily and with a steely resolve.

True to the inspired expectations of Mark Twain, the two-volume set went on to sell some 300,000 copies, and became a classic work of American literature. Ulysses S. Grant died on July 23, 1885, just as his memoirs were being published, at the age of 63. Ultimately, the work earned Grant's family nearly $450,000, or roughly $1,000,000 in today's dollars.

Grant's inspiration arose from a deep-felt need and moved him to pursue a mission which, in his case, was given greater urgency by his impending death and the fate of his loved ones. While you and I may not find ourselves in such dire straits, the value of giving ourselves to a "mission" and being sufficiently inspired to accomplish it will far outweigh any amount of mere "motivation".

So get inspired. Have a mission.

Does It Make You Happy?

"The purpose of life is not to be happy. It is to be useful, to be honorable, to be compassionate, and to have it make some difference that you have lived and lived well." — Ralph Waldo Emerson

Happiness is overrated.

A Google search for the term "happiness" brought me 199,000,000 results. The phrase "How to find happiness" got 137,000,000 hits. Amazon lists 32,423 titles with the term "happiness" searched for books.

Everyone wants to be happy it seems. Being happy at work is a huge theme in business literature, magazines, blogs and has sprung a number of cottage industries telling us all how to achieve it. Being happy as a business owner comes closely behind. (Apparently, if you're the boss, you aren't expected to be happy - or else the assumption is that you already ARE happy because you're the boss and they aren't!)

But what if "being happy" is not really a goal? What if happiness is a result? A benefit? A side-effect even? What if the point is not to pursue happiness - in the typical, contemporary and somewhat fleeting and shallow sense of the word as it is used today - but to pursue purpose and meaning? And what if happiness merely occurred for us we did so?

What if?

Do You Want To Be A Success?

Yeah, well, don't we all?

But as we make that statement (or some variation on it) we often fail to answer for ourselves the immediate question that is begging: What does that mean really? Success? And further more - and more to the point - what does that mean for me?

So, ask yourself, how exactly would you define success for YOU? What would you be doing if you were successful in your own mind? What does that look like for you? Lots of money? Big house? Three cars? Trips to St. Thomas every year?

Or is it more subtle and nuanced? For some, we know, success is simply getting through the day without dying. For most of us, however, it involves something that promises to gratify a longing and a desire for meaning, for purpose. It may involve money, but only because the money becomes an inevitable result of the success we seek.

But it may not really be about the money.

There are two points I want to make here (nothing profound or earth-shattering, sorry!):

1) We, each of us, must ultimately define and envision success for ourselves. What constitutes success for, say, Sir Richard Branson would not be success for me. Not my style, not where my heart is. And our understanding of and definition of success cannot be determined by strictly external rewards and trappings. We all know the truism that many rich people are miserable. Success comes from within.
2) We, each of us, must succeed for ourselves. No one can succeed for us. Remember, only you can prevent forest fires, as Smokey would say. Only you can do what must be done to achieve whatever it is that you have deemed to be "Success" for you. Circumstances and the odds may be against you - and the bitter reality is that no one of us has a guarantee of succeeding - but unless you make up your

mind and set your heart firmly and resolutely upon that goal, then failure WILL BE guaranteed.

Clarity of vision, singleness of purpose, and unwavering resolve - these are key elements of success.

So you want to be a success?

Sowing And Reaping

My ancestors were farmers. Almost every one of them. A few carpenters and merchants were thrown in there, but farming seemed to be the prevalent occupation of my forebears. Tillers of the land.

I was thinking about farming, and planting in particular, as I worked on a **marketing strategy**, and it occurred to me that the similarities are quite numerous. So I identified seven principles, or practices, in farming that could be applied to marketing and **lead generation**.

1. Plan. Farmers do not randomly throw seed around their fields and yards. Not only would it be chaotic, but the chickens would eat up a lot, as well as the other birds and critters. No, good farmers have a plan and a strategy before they even touch the soil or the seed.

2. Prepare. Ever walked on a fallow field? One that is hard, crusted over, rough and clotted with weeds? Not going to grow much with that. Preparation is essential for ensuring any chance of success when planting seed.

3. Plant. Yep! That's what has to follow. Lots of seed. More seed than you know will ever take hold and produce. And the funny thing about planting is that poor seed, if it takes, produces poor crops. Gotta have good seed and plenty of it.

4. Nurture. The weeds have to be pulled, the birds kept away, the other critters kept out, and plenty of water at the right times and in the right places. Nurture is a soft, pretty word for 'work'!

5. Patience. Once you have done everything you can do with a crop you can only do nothing except wait. This does not mean being inactive or sleeping till noon. There is always plenty to do on the farm. Different seed gets planted at different times. Some fields have to be furrowed while others are being harvested. But you cannot make the darn seed sprout and grow any faster. You gotta be patient.

6. Harvest. Payday! Eventually, if all goes well and you don't have drought or pestilence or evil bankers foreclosing on the farm, you will reap what you have sown. And the cool thing about the harvest is that each mature plant holds more seed. (think: referrals, repeat business, subscription sales, etc.)

7. Repeat. No one succeeds in farming with just one harvest. Farmers farm until they can't any more. (Or until some giant agricultural conglomerate buys the farm and the farmer retires and spends his winters in St. Thomas!)

So put on your overalls and your boots, grab a cup of coffee, and happy farming!

So You're In A Relationship

So this is not news, but to experience being a customer with many companies one would have to wonder. Regardless of how a business conducts itself, how it takes care of its customers (or not!), or how it functions in general, the inescapable fact is that there are relationships being formed.

They may be good, poor or mediocre. They be mutually beneficial or adversarial. They may even be co-dependent and dysfunctional! But it is still a relationship.

Until the customer goes somewhere else.
Losing a customer is the business equivalent of receiving a Dear John letter. Or not getting the letter and simply left wondering what happened. We could carry the metaphor too far with backbiting (negative word-of-mouth) and other sordid analogies, but the point is made, I think.

In a business we are in the business of relationships. With our customers, our employees, our vendors and suppliers, perhaps with our lenders, investors, or shareholders – and with the community in which we do business. There is no escaping it, no getting around it, or away from it.

Here are three steps, or actions, we need to build and maintain HUMAN relationships as a business:
1. Be Human - This can mean many things, but in this context it means being "real", authentic, caring, and confident: confident of who you are, what you have to offer, what you stand for, and why it matters.
2. Communicate - Words can be empty, but well-said words are valuable. Our actions communicate. Our branding, our values, our product or service - these all communicate. But above all else, we need to communicate clearly, competently, caringly, and consistently.
3. Connect - It's a truth we all know, but often forget - not everyone is your customer. Not every prospective customer is a good fit for you company, your purpose, your values. But there are those who

are. And you must connect with them, become "friends" with them, cultivate a community with them.

Too simple? Perhaps. But I challenge you to try it.

So why not embrace it?
When a business owner actually grasps and internalizes the truth that he or she is in the business of creating, building and nurturing relationships, the task of running a business takes on an entirely different perspective. As it should. And when this reality is imparted to the employees and integrated into the whole spectrum of functions and actions of the business – the transformation can be huge.

It is not a stretch to say that what might have been a simple commercial exchange between a customer and a business has the potential for being a life-changing event. Maybe not every time. Probably not most of the time. But each transaction, each interaction, each action that somehow touches a customer can be, and should be, an impactful one.

Build a business that no one wants to break up with.

Reach Out And Connect

Last night, I attended a quarterly networking event of a local **LinkedIn Group** that I belong to. It was, as always, fun and challenging. Fun, because the people are fun, the structure is enlivening, and the atmosphere is upbeat and informal.

Challenging, because meeting new people –*business* people - can bring out the Middle School wallflower in all of us. Well... most of us anyway. But I had to keep reminding myself that I was there for a reason and it was not solely self-serving nor completely altruistic. I was there because I need and want more relationships.

The unofficial mantra of our Group is *"Networking is not enough... Relationships are the key!"* And while I do appreciate the strategic value of effective networking, I also realize that things really happen for people as a result of a relationship with others.

People Helping People
So why do we need relationships birthed from networking and referrals? Here's my take:

1. You Need Others
You and I cannot do this all alone. On the most fundamental level we must have others to buy our products or services in order to even have a business. Beyond that, we need people to help us run our business, sell our stuff, do our bookkeeping, and so on. The world is full of people who can help. The last time I checked there were about **321,000,000** people in the U.S. alone. And the only way you can benefit from the help others can give is by having some kind of relationship with them. And the more, the better.

2. Others Need You
This is flip side of the coin, so to speak. You have value you can bring to others. And there are plenty who need it. If fact, you possess far more value to others than you may realize because it's not limited to your business, your products or services, or even your skills and knowledge. Because relationships have a way of drawing us out of

ourselves in ways we do not always anticipate. And we can do for others in ways we may not have ever imagined.

3. Needs Are Met In Relationships

And therein lies the rub - if I simply have your name and email address, or a profile and image on LinkedIn, or (possibly worse) a Twitter handle on my smart phone - then we are simply "connections". Can't have you over for coffee; you can't buy me lunch; and I doubt seriously if you're going to give me an unqualified referral to your mother!

But if we move beyond a mere connection and began establishing a relationship... well, then all kinds of good things can come about! I can help you, you can help me; we can both learn from each other, grow and stretch as people, possibly even become quite good friends - it is truly unlimited where a relationship can go.

Reach Out

I would suggest that if you have not already you need to look for and become a part of a group, an organization, a club - something! - that will allow you to reach out and make connections. And then nurture those connections until they become relationships.

We Are All Authors

J.M. Barrie once said, *"The life of every man is a diary in which he means to write one story, and writes another; and his humblest hour is when he compares the volume as it is with what he vowed to make it."*

Each day a page will be written in the story of your life.

How will you write it?

I Resolve

While it is customary to make New Year's resolutions, here is a perspective on lifelong resolutions that, upon reflection, are not that bad:

The Thirteen Virtues of Benjamin Franklin

Temperance. Eat not to dullness; drink not to elevation.

Silence. Speak not but what may benefit others or yourself; avoid trifling conversation.

Order. Let all your things have their places; let each part of your business have its time.

Resolution. Resolve to perform what you ought; perform without fail what you resolve.

Frugality. Make no expense but to do good to others or yourself; i.e., waste nothing.

Industry. Lose no time; be always employ'd in something useful; cut off all unnecessary actions.

Sincerity. Use no hurtful deceit; think innocently and justly, and, if you speak, speak accordingly.

Justice. Wrong none by doing injuries, or omitting the benefits that are your duty.

Moderation. Avoid extremes; forbear resenting injuries so much as you think they deserve.

Cleanliness. Tolerate no uncleanliness in body, cloaths, or habitation.

Tranquility. Be not disturbed at trifles, or at accidents common or unavoidable.

Chastity. Rarely use venery but for health or offspring, never to dullness, weakness, or the injury of your own or another's peace or reputation.

Humility. Imitate Jesus and Socrates.

From *The Autobiography of Benjamin Franklin*, (1791)

Getting The Word Out

In the course of building a business or a practice, one must engage in a certain amount of promotion. This can take the form of paid advertising, publicity, public relations, requesting referrals, generating positive word-of-mouth, and... using and leveraging social media.

It has become an axiom of sorts today that anyone with a business, a practice, a cause, must have a blog. And for a blog to be effective and truly useful it must be consistently posted to. In other words, the only way you are going to even hope to get people to come back and read what you write is to keep writing something worth reading.

Consistently. And every day. Or, at least, every week.

Are you a blogger?
It is said that about 300 words is the minimum - or maximum - you should post, depending on which social media guru you happen to subscribe to. 300 words at first glance seems to be quite nominal compared to, say, an 80,000 word book or even a 5,000 word white paper. Shoot! Three hunnert words ain't hardly nothin'!

Except when you sit day each day and look at the blank screen. Or your blank pad of paper. Or your blank brain...

And I am writing this not because I needed to fill some space or to find a way to complain about writing under the guise of pontificating. No, I am writing this because I believe that blogging - which is really just writing with an odd name - is terribly underrated by too many professionals and business owners.

Why blog anyways?
Writing and maintaining a blog is highly beneficial on a number of important levels:

1. It allows you to communicate directly to the people who matter the most in your business: your customers, clients, and prospects.

This is your opportunity day-in and day-out to express your heart, to share your knowledge, to give real value in digestible chunks.

2. Blogging forces you to think clearly, concisely and compellingly about what matters most: what your business does for people. Too many business owners and professionals have great difficulty communicating what they do for people - beyond the obvious. Too many of us are challenged to see our own products and services from a meta perspective. In other words, we are so in our own weeds we often can't see our meadow.

3. Writing a blog provides an opportunity to position yourself and your brand in the minds and hearts of your audience. The permanence and iniquitousness of the Internet can be dangerous, for sure, but also vastly beneficial and powerful for those with limited resources.

And then there is also the discipline factor: 300 words - or die! Nothing like accountability to keep one motivated.

Taking Care Of Business

"After all, the chief business of the American people is business. They are profoundly concerned with producing, buying, selling, investing and prospering in the world. I am strongly of the opinion that the great majority of people will always find these the moving impulses of our life."
- President Calvin Coolidge, 1925

It's just business

The founding of this country was initiated by the endeavors of a corporation whose sole intent was to establish a profitable business enterprise on the shores of the New World. The result of that first attempt eventually became Jamestown, Virginia. The enterprise failed, the colony almost did, and no one really made any money in the first round.

But the opportunities were too great to ignore.

America teemed with resources and there were many, many people whose entrepreneurial drive pushed them to risk all for the possibility of a profit. The actual term "entrepreneur" wasn't used until the mid-1800s, however. It was a French word that became an adopted English term for someone who undertook great risk with the aim of reaping a financial profit in the undertaking.

Opportunity meets motivation

It's been 400 years since John Rolfe, newly transplanted resident of Jamestown, Virginia, succeeded in growing a variety of tobacco there. The trade possibilities of this commodity were staggering the future of the colony - and what would eventually become the United States - was more or less assured.

And from these questionably auspicious beginnings, Americans have engaged in trade and entrepreneurialism ever since. And the risks never go away; the undertaking still requires blood, sweat and tears. But we love it!

So what is your undertaking? And where will you take your corner of our shared entrepreneurial legacy?

From Good To Great

Any business can be good.

A quality product, a good service offering, well-trained staff... it is relatively easy to be a good company. Even really good. And there are multitudes of them out there. Including yours.

But to become a truly *great* company... well, that is something else.

Knowing Greatness
"Great" is a slippery and somewhat relative term - kind of like "success" - but in this context it is not necessarily size, gross annual revenue, net profitability, or even being voted "Best Place To Work"! Yet these can all be hallmarks of a great business.

Greatness is a bit more sublime and intrinsic. Greatness transcends mercantile transactions and employee perquisites. It is more than company culture. It is what allows a business to create a lasting legacy, to positively impact the lives of many, and provides value far beyond the widgets or services it may provide.

And it is intentional.

Greatness doesn't just happen because someone made all the right decisions, the stars aligned, and the Universe happened to smile on that particular business. It happens because a leader made a conscious decision to build something great.

What have you decided?

Real Business

People do business with people.

Not "brands", or companies, or businesses. They may buy things online, but that isn't "doing business" - that's pressing buttons and pulling levers to get a mouse treat. I buy books (and other stuff!) through Amazon. But there is no interaction with a human, no relationship being conducted... not even a face.

It's more than just a mechanical transaction.

And while an impersonal series of transactions may accumulate corporate wealth for a company, it does not create a great business. A good "business model" perhaps, but not a "Great" business.

And that is what you are striving to build, isn't it? Something far more substantial, valuable, and fulfilling than simply a profitable enterprise? Perhaps in your vision for the future of your business you have thought about it in terms of a legacy even. You want to have an impact on the world, not just on your bottom line.

So you need to be real.

To be real means to be authentic, genuine, and heartful. It is not really all that easy or simple, but it is the difference between having a company that is simply "Business as usual" - just like the other guy - and a company that is truly great and that has an impact far beyond mercantile interests.

So why be real? Here's a few key reasons:

1. Being real is being authentic. Humans value authenticity over image. I know we live in a world that says "Image is everything." But, really, in the give-and-take of human relationships authenticity is what truly matters. And if your business, your "brand", your company culture exudes authenticity - even a gritty, imperfect genuineness - people will respond.

2. Being real means integrity. Doing what is right has always been a challenge for human beings. But doing the right thing as a business entity can be incredibly difficult at times. For integrity is an all-pervasive thing that must be evident internally as well as externally. Doing the right thing is what you must do for your customers and your employees and your community. Because people respect integrity.

3. Being real is being different. You are not that other guy. Your business is not that other business. *Even if you do the same thing and sell the same thing!* Listen: not everyone who could be your customer is your customer. If you are real you will not attract everyone. If you are real you will repel someone. Comes with the territory. So be comfortable with who you are and be that. Because there are plenty of people who *will* like you.

Oscar Wilde once said, *"Be yourself, everyone else is already taken."*

A Four-Letter Word

Okay, so DISCIPLINE is more than four letters. But it still lands like a bad word on most of us. Probably out of guilt, or an awkward acknowledgement that we need to exercise more of it. Either way, it doesn't sit well with many of us because... well, face it: most of us tend towards a lack of consistent discipline.

And where does it show up for business owners? My experience has been that it manifests itself in these three areas more often than not:

- Time management
- Self-organization
- Financial management practices
-

What's missing?
It's not so much a lack of planning, or tools, or intent: we often are, in fact, overloaded with these things. And we know (with a tinge of bitterness) that all the plans, tools, and good intentions will not cause us to be any more or less disciplined.

And it is the discipline is what makes the other things work.

So what to do? Without getting too psychoanalytical I would offer that the core motivation for maintaining business and operational discipline is key. Many employees maintain a level of discipline partly out of fear of "getting in trouble" and partly out of a desire to make more money, etc. A surprising number of previously unfit people suddenly become disciplined with their work-outs and exercise when they discover they are in danger of a heart disease! Motivation counts, and a proper motivation can make the difference between avoidance and commitment.

Motivate me!
There is a world of difference between knowing that something needs to be done because it's "better" to do it than to not do it, and knowing that doing it leads to vastly greater rewards. Discipline in key areas of life, particularly your business life, does lead to far

greater benefits - it is a question of keeping those benefits top of mind in the midst of the day-to-day grind.

And the benefits must be compelling and sufficiently valuable to us. Extending one's life span and postponing death is certainly compelling. Just losing a few pounds or feeling better about one's self may not be. Which is why so many people sign-up for gym memberships, but soon stop going. So the key is to have a motivation that transcends your resistance to doing the things you know you should be doing.

It is a truth that foregoing the pleasure of *not* planning your week and day (because it is not an enjoyable task!) will generate far greater returns later on. It is a fact that taking the time to get truly organized and *maintaining that state* will reap greater effectiveness, productivity, as well as increased focus and clarity. And staying on top of your financial management practices and tasks can literally prevent unanticipated fiscal disasters. Never mind increased visibility, awareness, and profitability.

Just Do It.
Whatever else Nike meant to communicate with their tagline, one thing is fundamentally true - discipline comes down to this: you just have to do it.

Easy to say, not so easy to actually practice. But once you have provided yourself with a truly compelling motivation (something verging on life or death!) it really is simply a matter of just "doing it".

Drill Bits Or Holes?

"What do you sell?" Jerry paused before answering the question. We were sitting in a small break-out group of business owners and entrepreneurs during a session at a business leadership seminar. The group leader had asked a simple question, "What do you sell?"

"My competition is not other landscape suppliers." Jerry began. His thriving business in the heart of the deep South provided building and landscape supplies and materials, as well as installed backyard barbecues and fireplaces. "My competition," he continued slowly, "are the airlines."

Eyebrows raised and a few group members chuckled uncertainly. Airlines? What did they have in common with landscapers and masonry suppliers?

Jerry continued, "I don't sell backyard barbecues or fire-pits. I sell an escape." Everyone listened intently now. "My customers are looking for a place to escape to from the pressures of work, of life, and they don't always want to have to leave home to have that. The airlines can give them that, but I can give it to them right there in the privacy of their own backyards - a personal get-a-way where they can escape to."

Jerry, with a quiet passion and firm conviction, had succeeded in building a solid business by seeing what it was that his customers were really buying from him. While the other stores like his in town were selling commodities, he was selling something far more.

You're probably not selling what you think you're selling.
As business owners it is far too easy to focus on the apparent, the obvious, and tell ourselves that we are selling a particular service or product. The automotive mechanic sells auto repairs. The shoe store sells shoes. And so on.

But what, really, is your customer buying? There is an old saying that no one really wants a half-inch drill bit. They want a half-inch hole. So even though they purchase the drill bit, what they are "buying" - what the hardware store sold them - is a half-inch hole.

What do your customers really want from you when they buy? What do they get that even they may not realize consciously?

That's the million dollar question. Because if you can nail that then you are already far and away past your competition.

So, what ARE you selling?

Why Your Meetings Suck

It's nothing new.

In most companies, in every country, regardless of their position, people hate meetings. And rightfully so.

The Meetings Will Continue Until Morale Improves

Business meetings can be so bad - and inescapable - that Patrick Lencioni, the founder of The Table Group, was able to write a best-selling book on the topic entitled *Death By Meeting*. And, yet, the bad meetings continue. Productivity suffers, or stalls. And people hate going to them.

But why is that?

I propose that there are probably a myriad of reasons working together in a toxic matrix that infects most meetings in most companies all over. But for the purposes of this blog post I want to focus in on the three main reasons why your meetings suck:

Reason #1 - They are boring

Face it: most of your meetings are not as exciting as the big box of donuts Susan from HR thought to bring in. Imagination, creativity, and novelty almost never see the light of day in a typical business meeting. I have sat through meetings where the most interesting thing said was, "Well, that about wraps it up. Any questions?"

But boring is a function of the leader, not the meeting. Meetings do not have to be, nor should they be BORING. But it takes a leader with the appropriate degree of awareness and preparation to conduct a business meeting that keeps people not only awake, but engaged and eager to do it again.

Reason #2 - They are unstructured

A big contributor to the boring-icity (new word!) of business meetings is the lack of structure. There should be a Federal statute against calling and conducting any meeting without an agenda. And I mean a bonafide business agenda that is on paper (or the digital equivalent thereof). Not some disenfranchised manager's twisted personal agenda...

How often have you sat through a meeting that ran off the rails onto tangents that meandered back (or didn't), were abruptly forced back, or simply disintegrated into some sort of vague free-for-all discussion? Meetings without a structure, an agenda, and a ruthlessly diligent timekeeper and chair will always be prone to going long, going shallow, and going nowhere.

Reason #3 - They are unproductive

And the third reason rides on the coattails of the previous reason. The end result of far too many business meetings is a lack of any tangible results. What in the heck did we actually accomplish in the last hour and a half?! A Wall Street Journal poll showed that CEOs list meetings as the single largest category of unproductive time on their schedules. And another study revealed that the average employee spends approximately 25% of their business days in meetings on average.

Just shoot me now.

But it isn't supposed to be that way!

Not according to Lencioni,

"There is nothing inherently boring or unproductive about meetings. They are the activity at the center of every organization, and should therefore be both interesting and relevant in the lives of participants. If we can just turn everything we know about meetings upside down - replace agendas and decorum with passion and conflict - we can transform drudgery into meaningful competitive advantage."

That's weighty stuff, but it is true. Our problem is that we have, for the most part, bought into the misconception that meetings are a necessary evil that we are wise to avoid, doomed to endure, and assume will always be that way.

But they don't have to.

Can't Buy My Love

What, exactly, are you hoping to achieve with your marketing efforts? A sale? A customer? A raving fan? All of these?

The obvious answer is "a sale", although the technically correct purpose of marketing is debatable. I Googled this question, "What is the purpose of marketing?" and got about 528,000,000 results (in only 0.39 seconds! And I would wager that there were about 528 different answers with a million versions.

So, what IS the purpose of marketing? Why do you do it?

Wise men say...
I would contend that, in addition to a number of other essential results, the primary purpose of your marketing is to win the hearts and minds of your customer.

The primary function of your marketing is to cause your prospective customers to fall in love with your brand and to keep them in love after they become customers.

And this objective involves every facet of your business. Everything you do becomes a marketing function when viewed through this rose-colored lens. Every stage of your sales cycle, customer life cycle, and business life cycle is intrinsically a part of marketing. Every function, every position, and every department – *everything* must work together to win and keep the hearts and minds of your customers.

It don't happen with one date
Far too many small businesses are short-sighted when it comes to marketing and the goal of winning a customer. Especially those who are engaged in one-off sales of products or services. They remind me of the guy who is great at getting a date with a new girl, but never has another chance with her because he quit romancing her after the first date. (Or worse, even *during* the date!)

Don't be that guy.

Just because I am enamored with your website, your offer, your sales staff... you are going to need to keep me entranced with your product or your service, and you will need to keep yourself top of mind once I have become your customer and enthralled with the value and attention you give me. And - most importantly - you must find ways to keep me wanting to come back for more and telling all my friends about you.

So - are you being romantic enough?

About the Author

Real Serious Stuff is the result of many years of observation and experience. I have worked for a number of companies over the years, both small (some very tiny!) and large (a few really big!), and have run my own business ventures, as well.

During that time I developed a passion for great customer service, great marketing, and great companies. Because of this, and the fact that small businesses create the majority of the jobs in our nation, I believe that small businesses have the potential for transforming our society by building and creating a culture of greatness. And this will be accomplished by how they "do business".

I am a certified business coach and worked with Michael E. Gerber's coaching company, EMyth, for over 7 years before moving out on my own journey as an independent coach specializing in Business Leadership.

You can visit my website at **www.BobbyBurnsCoaching.com**.

Passion and Purpose

My particular passion has led me to defining greatness as it applies to businesses. Inspired by Michael E. Gerber's The E-Myth Revisited, and other works, I have worked to help small business owners discover how to start, build, and sustain great companies. This goal is founded on the idea that the products or services being offered must themselves be great, and - just as importantly - that the companies that offer them want to be great. But it's not enough to simply desire to be great - *you must have the heart for it*!

"There is a difference between having 'desire' and having 'heart'."

Greatness, passion, and fun - these are all part of my work with small business owners and their employees. Yet, underlying all of this is the sobering truth that we are indeed engaged in real serious stuff.

To Inspire, Motivate, and Educate.

My goal - through business coaching, speaking, and writing - is to inspire business owners by motivating and educating them towards greatness.

Greatness does not always equate to size.

Big is not necessarily great. Highly profitable is not the same as great. Even being well known isn't great. As a small business owner, you must understand and believe that greatness resides within us first and foremost. Then it can be imparted into our businesses through leadership, culture, and a spirit of service. Greatness can reside in our employees, in the way we do business, and in how we are seen and experienced by our customers and our community.

Abraham Maslow believed that American businesses held the key to a truly transformative society if only we could learn to maximize the potential within each of our individual companies.

And that is why I call this Real Serious Stuff!

You can contact me at **bobbyrayburns@gmail.com**

REAL
SERIOUS
STUFF

IT'S WHAT YOU DO.

www.ingramcontent.com/pod-product-compliance
Lightning Source LLC
Chambersburg PA
CBHW051905170526
45168CB00001B/251